TELECOMMUNICATIONS IN TURMOIL
Technology and Public Policy

Gerald R. Faulhaber

BALLINGER PUBLISHING COMPANY
Cambridge, Massachusetts
A Subsidiary of Harper & Row, Publishers, Inc.

International Standard Book Number: 0-88730-157-6

Library of Congress Catalog Card Number: 87-1377

Printed in the United States of America

Library of Congress Cataloging-in-Publication Data

Faulhaber, Gerald R.
    Telecommunications in turmoil.

    Includes bibliographies and index.
    1. American Telephone and Telegraph Company—
Reorganization.   2. Telephone—United States.
3. Telecommunication—United States.   I. Title.
HE8846.A55F38   1987   384'.068   87-1377

ISBN 0-88730-157-6

For Jackie

Contents

Glossary of Acronyms ... xi
Preface ... xiii
Introduction ... xv

Chapter 1 Telecommunications as a Regulated Monopoly: Why It Worked ... 1
Technology Rewarded: The Bell Patents ... 1
Technology Redux: The Vail Strategy ... 2
Regulation: The New Game in Town ... 5
The Strategy Endures: Regulatory Developments ... 7
The Strategy Endures: Technological Developments ... 8
The Strategy Endures: The Roads Not Taken ... 11
The Strategy Endures: Market Developments ... 15
Notes ... 18
References ... 20

Chapter 2 The Regulated Monopoly Embattled: 1959–1974 ... 23
Private Microwave: The First Crack ... 24
The Cross-Subsidy Issue ... 25
Telephones and Terminals: Another Breach ... 27
Long-Distance: The Heart of the System ... 30
The Strategy Unravels: What Happened? ... 33
Notes ... 35
References ... 36

Chapter 3 The Regulators Embattled: 1959–1974 ... 39
A Digression: History and Theory of Regulation (Revised) ... 39
The Theory Applied: Bell's Regulatory Compact ... 45

The Compact Unravels   48
The FCC's Economists   50
The Datran Caper   50
The Bell Economists   53
On the Cusp of Change   54
Notes   55
References   56

Chapter 4 The Policy Debate Engaged: 1974–1981   59
New Initiatives   59
A New Initiative from Bell   60
The Control of Cross-Subsidy   64
A Stake in the Heart of the System   67
The Structuralists Strike Again: Resale and Arbitrage   69
Access: The Nub of the Problem   72
The Bell Response   76
Notes   78
References   79

**Chapter 5 The Debate Resolved: The Divestiture
          Decision**   81
The Machineries of Justice, Continued   81
The Fateful Decision   83
Greene Takes Control   84
Divestiture is NOT Deregulation   85
The Theory of the Case: How It Might Have Worked   87
The Theory of the Case: How It Might Have Failed   89
Denouement: Judge Greene Cuts a Deal   96
Notes   101
References   102

Chapter 6 The Economics of Telecommunications   105
The Economics of Regulated Monopoly   105
The Economics of Antitrust   115
Notes   125
References   125

Chapter 7 Life After Divestiture: Facing the Future   127
The Struggle for the Market   128
The Children of Divestiture   136
The Regulatory Game, Once Again   139
Notes   147
References   148

**Chapter 8 The Future of Telecommunications: An
              Immodest Proposal**   151
Industry Prospects   151
Regulation Is the Problem, Not the Solution   159
An Immodest Proposal   164
Conclusion   174
Notes   175
References   176

Index   179
About the Author   187

Glossary of Acronyms

AT&T-C   AT&T-Communications. The division of AT&T, incorporating the former AT&T Long Lines, established to manage all long-distance communications, both inter- and intrastate. Pursuant to the FCC's ruling in the Third Computer Inquiry, this division was permitted to merge with AT&T-IS.

AT&T-IS   AT&T-Information Systems. The division of AT&T established as a separate subsidiary to engage in competitive businesses, under the FCC's Second Computer Inquiry rules. Pursuant to the FCC's ruling in the Third Computer Inquiry, this division was permitted to merge with AT&T-C.

BOC   Bell Operating Company. Any of twenty-two companies providing local exchange services to specific franchised geographic areas under regulation. These companies have been grouped into seven regional holding companies, which also own other nonexchange enterprises.

CPE   Customer Premises Equipment. Any and all telephone equipment, generally located on the premises of the customer, connected to the telephone network.

FSS   Fully Separated Subsidiary. In its Second Computer Inquiry, the FCC permitted the Bell System to engage in competitive businesses only through subsidiaries that were "arm's length," or fully separated, from the firm's primary business in monopoly markets.

MCI   Microwave Communications, Inc. The earliest and most successful of the competitive long-distance carriers.

MFJ   Modification of Final Judgement. The 1982 agreement (consent decree) between AT&T and the Department of Justice specifying the terms of the divestiture. This was entered, not as an independent consent decree, but as a modification of the consent decree that terminated the 1956 AT&T-Justice antitrust case.

PBX   Private Branch Exchange. A switching device on the premises of a customer with many lines, permitting interconnection among those lines, as well as connection to the the nationwide network.

SBS   Satellite Business Systems. A now-defunct long-distance carrier, established as a joint venture among IBM, Comsat, and Aetna.

STS   Shared Tenant Services. An arrangement whereby telephone and other communication and computer services are offered to tenants of a building, office park, or condominium by a firm not operating under a regulated franchise. The firm provides connections to the local exchange companies, as well as connections to a long-distance carrier, and may offer other services as well.

Preface

Telecommunications in Turmoil is about the tumultuous past, present, and future of the telecommunications industry, an industry that touches nearly everyone in this country and defies the understanding of even the wisest thinkers. This book is one person's view of a still-unfolding story about which honest men differ strongly, and which may be rendered obsolete by tommorow's events.

This is also a book that reflects the experiences of its author, and I owe you, the reader, an accounting of those experiences. In 1962, I started a career at Bell Laboratories, working first in systems engineering and then in economics research. After transferring to American Telephone and Telegraph in 1978, where I directed microeconomic studies and later strategic planning and financial management, I left Bell in 1983 to accept an academic appointment. My years at Bell coincided with the long and involved policy debate that started with an industry dominated by a powerful regulated monopoly and ended with the irrevocable dissolution of the Bell System through court-ordered divestiture.

During those years, I subscribed to the same technology-based service ethic that every Bell employee believed in: the telephone company held a public trust, and our every action should be motivated by service to the public. And yet, as a professional economist, I also understood that successful firms constantly struggle to maximize their financial returns, subject to technological and regulatory constraints that they as constantly struggle to loosen. In fact, these two views formed the undercurrent of the policy debate: was Bell the "gentle giant" it claimed to be, serving only the public interest, or was it a greedy monopolist, masking its cunning with the cant of public service? Nearly all of the participants in the policy debate could identify (however unprofessionally) with one or the other of these views. With me, the debate took place inside my head. I leave it to the reader to decide whether the view of my firm or that of my profession prevailed in this internal debate.

I am fortunate that so many of my friends and colleagues, whose comments reflected the extreme diversity of opinion on the subject, gave so generously of their time and critical faculties on an earlier draft. My heartfelt thanks (in alphabetical order) to: Dr. Alan Baughcum, R.W. Beck Associates; Professor William Baumol, Princeton University and New York University; Carolyn Burger, Assistant Vice-President of Bell of Pennsylvania; Edward Goldstein, the MAC Group; Alfred Kahn, Cornell University; Jack Mac-Allister, Chairman of U.S. West; Professor Roger Noll, Stanford University; Professor Almarin Phillips, University of Pennsylvania; Professor Lester Taylor, University of Arizona; Professor Leonard Waverman, University of Toronto; Professor John Wenders, University of Idaho; Professor Dennis Yao, University of Pennsylvania; and Professor Edward Zajac, University of Arizona. Acknowledging the help of others does not absolve the author of responsibility for errors, omissions, and plain dumb mistakes, which I hereby assume.

The initial inspiration for this book project came from Marjorie Richman of Ballinger Publishing, who had the wit to sniff out a story waiting to be told and the light touch needed to keep her author on track.

My deepest appreciation I owe to my wife, Jackie. The decision to go forward with the book was made with her, and the extensive burden of library research was borne by her. Her encouragement, support, and love sustained me through my long hours at the word processor; her substantive research efforts were essential to the quality of the book.

Philadelphia, Pennsylvania
December 5, 1986

Gerald R. Faulhaber

Introduction

Our nation is now embarked on an economic and technological experiment unprecedented in our (or anyone else's) history: the radical restructuring of the telecommunications industry, through the breakup of the old Bell system and the breakdown of barriers to new entry. We have taken what was by any measure the world's most technically advanced and productively efficient telephone system and turned it on its head.

Why did we do this? Was this supposed to be a good idea? What could we have been thinking of? All of us who have lived through the last year or so of confusion, crossed signals, and rising telephone prices are still waiting for the vaunted benefits that divestiture and deregulation were supposed to bring. What were they, and where are they?

Obviously, such a drastic solution could only have been the remedy to quite a serious problem, one that most Americans didn't know we had. In order to understand the nature of this problem, we shall trace the important technological, economic, and political currents in telecommunications and related industries that led to the initial policy debates of the 1960s. We will then explore the issues involved in the policy struggles of the 1970s and the roles of the various actors as the technological imperatives and economic forces were played out in Congress, the FCC, and the courts.

In the early part of this century, the Bell System put into place a business strategy that pulled together technology, politics, and economics to forge the world's largest and strongest private corporation. Chapter 1 describes how this strategy succeeded for over fifty years and lays the foundation for understanding the economic and political struggles that unraveled it.

The seeds of these struggles were sown by the revolution in electronic technology that occurred during and after the Second World War. The development of this technology, much of it from the fertile genius of Bell Laboratories, enabled other firms to supply customers with products and services in competition with Bell. The only barrier was regulatory, and firms seeking entry into telephone markets aggressively pressed their cases before regulatory commissions. As the opportunities for profit grew, so did the pressure on commissions to permit entry into the then monopoly Bell markets. Chapter 2 is the story of mounting force and counterforce, of competitors' offense and Bell's defense, of regulatory struggle.

If the battleground was regulatory, how did it shape the outcome of the battle? Only recently have political scientists and economists revealed the true nature of regulation: a deadly serious game for the highest of economic stakes. In Chapter 3, we review this developing theory and apply it to see how the fight to win the telecommunications regulatory game determined the role of competition in the telecommunications marketplace.

Slowly, but inexorably, the regulatory barriers gave way before the pressure of firms and consumers who wanted the benefits of competition. By the late 1970s, the mood of the nation was procompetitive and antiregulatory, and Bell's arguments sounded less and less compelling. In Chapter 4, we find the pace of the public policy debates quickening to a rush. Bell's attempts to preserve its traditional regulated monopoly were doomed.

The climax of this decade and more of public conflict was the divestiture agreement between AT&T and the Department of Justice, announced January 8, 1982. Essentially, AT&T acceded to the Justice Department's terms for structural change, in return for which Justice dropped its case. Clearly, the economists and lawyers in the Justice Department believed that the changes they sought would result in a more efficient, more effective, more innovative telecommunications system for the nation. But Justice's blueprint for the industry was not to be. The presiding judge, Harold Greene, had his own view of what was right, and seized control of the settlement process to impose that flawed vision on the industry. In Chapter 5, we examine the terms Justice sought, and why they sought them. Did Justice's theory of the case make sense? What were its defects? We'll see how the court derailed that plan, putting in its place a patchwork of restrictions with no coherence. As a result, on January 1, 1984, the day of divestiture, we opened the door to a Great Unknown.

To comprehend the divestiture decision and the impact of the settlement, we review the underlying economics of regulated monopoly and of antitrust in Chapter 6. What was regulation supposed to have accomplished in telecommunications, and how well did it do? What were the perceived antitrust problems in the industry, and did they pose a serious threat to the consumers of telephone service? Basic economic logic helps us sort out reality from rhetoric in this contentious and confusing area, and provides the basis for understanding what has happened in the industry since divestiture.

It is the peculiar genius of the American people that they are not deterred by the fact that they don't know what's going on. If the policy process brought us to a divestiture that left us all up in the air, then the right response seemed to be to keep doing our jobs and see what happens. In Chapter 7, we find out what has happened since divestiture. How did markets evolve? What did regulators do? How are the new players acting? What does this tell us about the underlying political and economic forces at work?

In Chapter 8, we review the prospects for the industry and find that the major obstacle to performance is continued regulation. We suggest that this problem can be solved and put forward an outline for deregulation that embodies consumer protections against the abuse of monopoly power and inefficiencies that regulation has always promised but never delivered.

It is sobering in the extreme to realize that our nation embarked upon this radical economic and political transformation with no hard evidence that it would work and with an incomplete theory of the experiment, which in any case was thoroughly scuttled by the one person who could take it upon himself to make it work. It is even more sobering to realize that this particular recklessness was the result of a public policy process that is still unfolding today, with the same people and institutions in charge. Nor can this public policy failure be attributed to the incompetence of the players; the best economists, lawyers, managers, engineers, and scientists participated in the debates and formulation of issues and solutions. Despite the efforts of our best minds, and regardless of the eventual outcome, our public policy process launched this country on a blind experiment in telecommunications. Does this experience tell us something about the effectiveness of the process by which our nation conducts its business? In a pluralistic, democratic society such as ours, is government part of the solution or part of the problem? Is the resolution of complicated issues, involving the interplay of technology, economics, and politics, simply beyond the competence of public policy today? This book deals with the failure of public policy in one industry, telecommunications, and drawing inferences on the basis of a sample of a single issue would be presumptuous in the extreme. Nevertheless, the ability of public policy to deal with complex social and economic problems, though beyond the scope of this book, is perhaps the deepest and most profoundly disturbing question raised by the events described.

CHAPTER 1

Telecommunications as a Regulated Monopoly: Why It Worked

Technology Rewarded: the Bell Patents

The telecommunications industry is more directly and specifically a child of technology than almost any other industry. The discovery and patenting of the telephone by Alexander G. Bell in 1876 marked simultaneously the birth of the technology and the birth of the business. Bell, the quintessential nineteenth-century tinkerer, quickly lost interest in his invention. He used the considerable proceeds from the sale of rights to his invention to spend the rest of his life, well, tinkering: with airfoils, hydroplanes, and a variety of other techno-toys of the day. His financial backers, however, recognized the value of his invention, and fought more than six hundred court battles over Bell's patent rights, not the least with the famous inventor, Thomas A. Edison (Goulden 1968: 37; Boettinger 1983: 98). Eventually having secured those rights, the American Bell Telephone Co. proceeded to exploit them successfully until their expiration in 1893 and 1894.

Of course, this is exactly how the patent system translates technical inventiveness into economic improvement. The inventor is granted exclusive use of his invention for a limited period of time, during which his ability to set price above cost generates a reward for his invention. This reward is the bait society offers the ingenious to induce them to inventive effort; the more useful or desirable the invention, the greater the reward. After the initial period, the invention becomes available to all, and the resulting competition forces price down to costs, increasing the benefits to consumers, but ending the flow of profits to the patent holders. Indeed, when the Bell patent ran out in the 1890s, hundreds of competitors entered existing markets and opened new ones, competing down the price of exchange service and capturing great chunks of market share from the less-than-nimble incumbent. By 1902, independent telephone companies served 44 percent of the market, and by 1907 their market share had increased to 51 percent (Bornholz and Evans 1983: 12). The competitive advantage granted by the original Bell patent was lost.

The management of American Bell Telephone had made no provision to replace that advantage. During its period of patent protection, high profits could have supported efforts to build a new technological edge to sustain the firm in later years. However, nothing was done to ensure that the expiration of the patent did not lead to the expiration of American Bell Telephone.

By the turn of the century, the nascent Bell System had fallen on parlous times. Bell's return on investment fell from an average of 46 percent during the term of patent protection to an average of 8 percent in the period of 1900–1906, a time of lower real interest rates (Bornholz and Evans 1983: 25). The early switching and transmission technology proved easy to duplicate and deploy. Many cities and towns were served by non-Bell companies; in many larger cities, competing systems, Bell and independent, existed side by side. The financial position of Bell deteriorated until, in 1907, it "fell into the hands of the bankers," in particular, J. P. Morgan, whose syndicate owned $90 million in unsold AT&T bonds (Bornholz and Evans 1983: 12). AT&T, successor holding company to American Bell, reorganized its Board of Directors, and Morgan's allies put Theodore Vail, a gifted manager and financier, at the helm.

Technology Redux: the Vail Strategy

Much has been written about the turnaround that Vail worked at Bell: how Vail used the newly emerging long-distance service (based on the loading coil, a technological advance that permitted transmission of analog electrical signals over much greater distances than previously possible) as a competitive weapon against the independents by refusing to connect their exchange territories to the new long-distance network; how this led to the purchase of many of the most profitable independents; how Vail met the upsurge of state regulation with accommodation and the development of the shared goal of "universal service"; how Vail shaped the corporate strategy—financial, regulatory, technological—for the Bell system for the next sixty years (Brock 1981: Chapter 6).

The linchpin of Vail's strategy was to gain control of the technology. Prior to the turn of the century, long-distance service was high cost and low quality, primarily due to the primitive methods of transmitting a voice signal. Subscribers in Boston talked to those in New York over thick, expensive copper wires—and they could hardly hear each other. Consequently, early telephone development concentrated on connections within an exchange, or several contiguous exchanges, covering a town or city. Most exchange networks were not able to speak with one another. The advent of reliable, cheap long-distance came with the loading coil of Pupin and Campbell, and later deForest's "audion," a forerunner of the vacuum tube. Vail made sure that the Bell System owned that technology (Fagen 1975: 243–244, 259–261). This allowed Bell to deploy a high-quality long-distance system that gave its subscribers much more value than the subscribers of the independent telephone companies received, permitting Bell to outcompete them.[1] By refusing to interconnect the independents, Vail created the conditions for Bell's profitable expansion by acquisition.

To understand the power of Vail's strategy, let's work through a simplified example.[2] Suppose that in 1912 Smalltown Telephone Company had 2000 subscribers in Smalltown, Indiana, where it competed directly with a Bell company that likewise served 2000 customers. Both companies had similar rates, enabling them to clear $1.00 per month over operating expenses per customer. The value of each company's future earnings (net present value of $2000 per month, discounted at 5 percent annually) would be $480,000. Assuming that each firm had $400,000 invested in switches, lines, and poles, both Smalltown Telephone and Bell had turned each dollar invested into $1.20 of value, a happy prospect for their share owners.

Now, what happens when Bell offers its new long-distance service? Suppose that three-quarters of the customers in Smalltown, Indiana, were willing to pay as much as $3.00 more per month to subscribe to this new service at Bell's rates (which in themselves were no doubt quite profitable), while the remaining quarter were purely local callers and did not value long-distance at all. Since Bell will not permit Smalltown Telephone to connect its customers to the long-distance network, Smalltown's local-only service will

instantly become less valuable to the three-quarters of its customers that value long-distance.

What are the options open to Smalltown Telephone? It can lower
its monthly rates by $3.00 in order to keep its current customers.[3]
If it does so, however, it will lose money on each subscriber, and
the business will be a loser. Alternatively, Smalltown can keep its
rates as before, lose the 1500 customers who value long-distance
to Bell, and with luck, attract the 500 customers who don't care
about long-distance. The best that Smalltown Telephone could do,
in this instance, would be to maintain its rates (and profit margin),
but reduce its subscriber base by half. The value of the firm's future cash flow would also be cut in half, from $480,000 to $240,000.
What previously looked like a good investment of $400,000 in tele-
phone plant and equipment for Smalltown Telephone would now
be a disaster: a $1 investment in Smalltown would now only be
worth 60 cents!

There is one more option for Smalltown Telephone: accept Bell's
offer to be acquired at $250,000. Clearly, Smalltown can expect no
better offer, since the value of its business is less than that, and
this would be the option it would have to choose.

When Bell acquires Smalltown Telephone, it acquires $400,000
of assets at the distress-sale price of $250,000. Even better, it dou-
bles the value of its new asset simply by connecting the system
to its long-distance network! After all, it was Smalltown's lack of
access to long-distance that caused its asset value to drop from
$480,000 to $240,000. When Bell integrates Smalltown customers
into its long-distance network, the asset value will go right back
up to its former level.[4]

This acquisition process possessed a cumulative aspect unique
to the telephone business. As Bell added more customers via acquisition, the value of the long-distance network service increased,
because more people could be reached. As the customer base grew,
the value of subscribing to it grew apace. And as that value grew, so
did Bell's ability to outcompete its rivals and its leverage to buy out
its competitors cheaply. The more acquisitions Bell made, the easier and cheaper were later acquisitions. Non-Bell companies who
anticipated this had incentive to sell out early, before the Bell steam-
roller built up momentum.

Why couldn't the independents match Bell's competitive advantage? Since the independents were denied access to Bell's long-

distance service, the independents could only match Bell if they could build their own. At the time, an independent spokesperson stated that "every one of us will acknowledge that our success or failure depends in a great measure upon whether or not we heed the many pleas made for better long-distance lines" (Houk 1905: 181–183). But Bell alone owned the dominant technology (the loading coil and, later, deForest's audion) that made long-distance work, and they were not about to license it to their competitors. The independents' efforts to build their own long-distance networks were doomed. It was the business genius of Vail that translated Pupin's loading coil into the marketplace muscle that created the Bell System. Ownership of the technology in the form of patent control gave Bell the economic leverage to climb from its dire straits of 1907 to its powerhouse position of 1913, the period of rapid growth through acquisition that marked the early Vail era.

But Vail did more than capture the then current technology. He had seen how the failure to plan for technology control had placed the firm in jeopardy, and he was determined never again to lose the technological edge necessary to win in the industry. Not only must the necessary technology be bought, but Bell must be in the forefront of creating it. Bell had hired its first Ph.D. physicist in 1885, but it was Vail who established the Bell tradition of organized scientific research that has kept it in the vanguard of technological innovation ever since (Fagen 1975: 37–45).

Regulation: The New Game in Town

An equally important component of Vail's strategy dealt with the growing social, political, and legal opposition to large corporations and "trusts." Popular disenchantment with the wealth and power of monopolists at the end of the nineteenth century culminated in antitrust legislation in 1890. In 1911, John D. Rockefeller was humbled by the *United States v. Standard Oil* case decision to dismember his firm. In 1913, antitrust was strengthened by the passage of the Clayton Act. Clearly, Vail's strategy of rapid acquisition and monopolization in the telephone industry ran straight into the teeth of prevailing popular sentiment and political will. In fact, in 1912, the Justice Department threatened to bring an antitrust suit against Bell on the grounds of its aggressive monopolization strategy; at the same time, the Interstate Commerce Commission launched an investigation of AT&T's practices (Bornholz and Evans 1983: 7–40).

In other industries in the United States, the problem of monopoly was being solved, not by breaking up the enterprise, but through public regulation. The newly emerging electric power industry, characterized by huge sunk costs, was seen as a "natural monopoly," in which competitive markets would not work. The solution—government regulation by "expert" commissions free of partisan political bias.[5] By 1910, both New York and Wisconsin had functioning state regulatory bodies, established to control rates, investment, entry, and exit for public utilities (Anderson 1980: 3–41).

Vail's response to these political currents was novel for the times: accommodation. Unlike Rockefeller, whose struggles against the tide ended with the dissolution of his oil empire, Vail chose to ride with the tide. If state regulators sought to control the profits of Bell companies in their jurisdiction, then he would accommodate them. If the Justice Department took him to court because he acquired too many telephone companies, he would voluntarily agree to cease such acquisitions, via the Kingsbury Commitment.[6]

Indeed, Vail did more than accommodate; he attempted to forge a partnership with the public sector. Bell would submit to and cooperate with regulation, including price, service quality, and rate-of-return regulation, in return for which the regulators would prohibit entry and let Bell operate as a regulated monopoly, managed as an "end-to-end" service, with no "foreign attachments," that is, other manufacturers' telephones (AT&T 1910: 33). Vail articulated a corporate and social goal that appealed to regulators, telephone executives, and customers alike: the universal availability of reliable, affordable telephone service, dubbed "universal service." Vail's slogan, announced in 1908, was One Policy, One System, Universal Service (Paine 1921: 238). Until the 1970s, this was the touchstone of all legal, regulatory, technical, and managerial decisions in telecommunications.

By 1915, Vail's strategy was fully formed and in place: maintain complete control over the market by (1) owning the technology needed for competitive success and (2) working in partnership with government to close off entry by other firms. Neither action was costless; by 1915, both AT&T and Western Electric, its manufacturing arm, maintained very large research, development, and engineering departments, precursors of Bell Laboratories.[7] In addition, to accommodate to regulation, Bell accepted potentially lower profit rates (commensurate with lower risk) and generally less control over its business.

The Strategy Endures: Regulatory Developments

The strategy survived Vail's death in 1920 and saw the Bell System through changing times. Virtually every state adopted some form of public utility commission to regulate telephone service.[8] After some years of perfunctory control by the ICC, federal regulation of all interstate electrical communication, including telephone, telegraph, and radio, was vested in the Federal Communications Commission (FCC) by the Communications Act of 1934, during the heyday of regulatory activity. Through all these changes, Bell's political strategy was constant: the social goal is universal service, and the regulator's role is to keep out competitors and to ensure an adequate return to Bell. Bell used the regulatory process quite diligently to maintain its control. Any attempt by a competitor to introduce a new telephone device or service to consumers was met with regulatory action by Bell.[9]

The goal of universal service with regulated monopoly was not without its detractors. While the Bell System of the 1920s and 1930s was considered by many to be the very model of a modern corporation, some were highly suspicious of its size and power. Shortly after the FCC was established, an investigation into the Bell System was launched by its Telephone Division under Commissioner Paul A. Walker. A proposed report of the Walker investigation was issued by the FCC in 1938, excoriating the Bell System and even suggesting nationalization as an alternative to what Walker saw as unworkable regulation.[10] The report focused attention on the relationship between Western Electric, Bell's manufacturing arm, and the operating units of the system. It noted that, since Western was unregulated, it could charge high prices for the capital goods purchased by the operating units, thus artificially inflating the value of their rate bases. The operating units could then justify rate increases, while appearing to adhere to cost minimization.

The Walker report was vilified by the press as "unfair," "one-sided," and a "travesty." The FCC quickly walked away from it, even to the point of abolishing its Telephone Division. However, the apparently radical ideas first expressed in the report could not be abolished, resurfacing later in the 1949 antitrust suit brought by the Justice Department against Bell. In that suit, Justice sought divestiture of Western Electric on much the same grounds that Walker, a decade previous, had faulted the vertical relationship between the operating companies and Western. Bell vigorously defended its vertically integrated structure and subsequently sought an accommodation with the Eisenhower administration that would not involve a Western Electric spin-off. In 1956, AT&T and Justice signed a consent decree that permitted Bell to keep its vertically integrated manufacturing arm, but at the cost of (1) freely licensing its Bell Labs technology and (2) restricting its business to only regulated utility operations (*United States v. Western Electric Company, Inc., et al.* 1956). It would be another two decades before Bell realized what it had paid to keep its vertical structure.

Nevertheless, Vail's strategy endured. Attacks on the social compact of universal service and regulated monopoly met with little public or political support. Regulators across the country fought with Bell on rate-base/rate-of-return issues, but apparently did not seriously question the basic structure of the telecommunications industry.

The Strategy Endures: Technological Developments

While Vail was establishing a preeminent technological position for Bell in long-distance telephone transmission, engineers and scientists were making exciting discoveries in the new field of radio, or "wireless".[11] The second decade of the twentieth century saw many fundamental advances in vacuum tubes, the core technology for not only radio but long-distance telephony as well. Efficient vacuum tubes could only be produced if each of the latest inventions were incorporated in the design. Since patent rights for these advances were held by a number of competing firms, the industry was in virtual patent gridlock regarding radio development.

The gridlock was broken in 1920 when the major parties signed a cross-licensing agreement (Reich 1977). AT&T, General Electric, and GE's recent offspring, the Radio Corporation of America, signed an agreement permitting each party the right to use the patents of the others, but limiting the market to which each party could apply the technology. Some 1200 patents were covered by this pact. Westinghouse was included in the agreement in 1921, and in 1926 the contract was renegotiated to exclude Bell from the newly emergent radiobroadcast business in return for which AT&T's exclusive hold over the wire telephony and radiotelephony public-network market was strengthened.

The cross-licensing agreement left Bell free to focus on the development and application of electronics for telephony without fear of competitive challenge from other American firms that owned the necessary technology. After 1926, telephony's major technical problem was the development of cheap, reliable transmission capacity, but the advent of coaxial cable and microwave radio after World War II brought enormous reductions in the cost of high-quality transmission.[12] The primary technical problem then became switching: the art and science of the systems that connect circuits and people together. In both these fields, the Bell system, operating since 1925 through its R&D subsidiary of Bell Telephone Laboratories, stood alone among commercial enterprises in its creation and control of the technology. Since Bell had both a legal monopoly, granted by regulation, and a technological monopoly, granted by the 1926 cross-licensing agreement, there seemed little reason for others to contribute to technology they couldn't use for themselves.

The characteristics of telecommunications technology were indeed unique. Because the components of telephony were defined — a telephone instrument, transmission, and switching — Bell Laboratories could focus on innovations to reduce the costs of existing products and services (*process* innovation) rather than on innovations of new products and services (*product* innovation).[13] Still, telecommunications technology has an important systems aspect that is often overlooked — all pieces of the system must work together at close tolerances. An important part of telecommunications R&D is "systems engineering" (Fagen 1978: 618), which determines not only whether individual parts work, but how they work together as a system. Yet another noteworthy factor is that capital facilities in telecommunications have very long physical lives (Jackson 1984: 79–81). Rapid uncontrolled technological innovation could render obsolete equipment whose useful lives were not over and whose costs had not been fully recovered from rates. Therefore, control over the process and timing of innovation was critical to the firm in order to reduce the risk of unanticipated technological advance and protect the profitability of sunk assets. But the technology was "isolated" under the 1926 agreement, and university research in the area was not extensive. Bell could afford to relax and concentrate on its specific needs. The result: "Bell Laboratories has dominated and continues to dominate research and development in telecommunications" (Zajac 1976).

All of these characteristics of technological advance in the Bell System during its period of regulated monopoly had important implications for the conduct of its business. The 1926 cross-licensing agreement permitted Bell to take advantage of Bell Labs' ability to generate patents. Since Bell had little to fear from other firms in competition for its markets, it engaged in a fairly active patent trade with other firms (Fagen 1975: 382–383). In this way, Bell could gain access to technology it needed by trading patent rights to firms that were not potential competitors. By 1935, Bell owned 9,255 patents outright and was licensed under 6,000 patents owned by others (Brock 1981: 173). Bell's concentration on process innovation was reflected in its manufacturing strategy, focused on the mass-produced high-reliability products associated with the Bell System, the most familiar being the old rotary-dial "500" telephone set. New products typically had the same function as the old; they just did it better and cheaper. The need for a marketing department is nil with such a strategy, and indeed Bell's interest in marketing was nil. An oft-quoted example of Bell's attitude toward marketing comes from an article by two Bell Labs' computer scientists: "A good product can find its way without marketing; indeed it may be the better for having no marketing concerns to drive it" (Kernighan and Margan 1982).

The necessity of a systems approach to telecommunications led Bell to develop the technology of "systems engineering," which later was applied outside the industry in large defense and aerospace projects. In the early years of the space program, Bell was asked to establish a subsidiary (Bellcomm) whose sole purpose was the systems engineering of the Apollo project (Fagen 1978: 673–675).

The preference of regulators for long-lived plant with long depreciation lives—which postpones the recovery of costs to future customers rather than today's electorate—coincided with the need to protect the firm against entry by unanticipated innovation, which could destroy the market value of capital assets in the field. It also fit well with the professional bias of technologists to design and build "bullet-proof" systems with thirty to fifty year lives.

Again, we see the subtle interplay among technology, economics, and regulatory politics. Bell itself created and owned the technology that made telephony better, faster, and cheaper. Even without regulatory barriers, Bell's control of the technology would have made it an imposing competitor, and few potential rivals would have risked entry. And that technology led to a highly capital-intensive, sunk-cost firm, with a high degree of interdependence of all its parts. It seemed that the very nature of the technology discouraged competition and demanded unitary system control, almost forcing the market to a monopoly solution, as Vail had advocated.

And yet the political influence on the technology, while indirect, was strong. Regulation seemed to lead Bell away from new products and services and towards improvements in its traditional telephone business. It seemed to push in the direction of long depreciation lives, with the attendant low rates for customers today, and thus reinforced the need for regulatory protection against future entry to protect the value of Bell's assets. The shared social objective of universal service of low-cost reliable telephone service, overseen by regulators and implemented by Bell, appears to have determined the shape of technological advance.

The Strategy Endures: The Roads Not Taken

As might be expected, such a single-minded focus on a specific social and regulatory goal can seriously distort the incentives and perceptions that would be normal in a more competitive industry. These distortions can lead a firm to take actions competitive industries generally avoid,[14] but the reverse is equally common, and as important. Of course, we can never find hard evidence that a firm did *not* take certain actions that a competitive firm would have taken. We can only look for "missed opportunities," situations in which our judgment tells us a competitive firm would have acted, but the regulated firm did not. In the case of the Bell System, an illustration of such a missed opportunity might be its response to the potential of television.

In the immediate postwar era, television became one of the nation's most vigorous growth industries (along with telephones). The growth of television required the simultaneous growth of several subindustries: the manufacture of TV sets; programming and broadcasting; and intercity distribution of network TV signals. In the industry's early stages, it was subject to "adoption external-ities"—the value of each activity depended on the existence of other firms carrying out the complementary activities.[15] This is quite similar to the problem in telephone networks, wherein the value of a single telephone to a single consumer is zero, but as more telephones are added to the network, the value of each phone increases. In the latter case, Bell had made the argument that the only way to overcome this problem was through a regulated mo-nopoly committed to the social goal of universal service.

No such argument was made regarding television, and each seg-ment of the industry developed with different firms. Zenith, Emer-son, RCA, and others manufactured and distributed sets, while the major radio networks transformed themselves into TV networks. However, it was the Bell System that provided the capability of long-haul transmission of TV signals, without which, TV would have remained a local broadcast phenomenon.

Why Bell? Technology, of course! Fundamental research from Bell Labs in the 1930s on FM radio was brought to bear on defense problems of World War II, leading to the development of reliable microwave communications. Directly after the war, the Bell Sys-tem began a microwave construction program, linking the two coasts by 1949. This transmission capability was to be used not only for the newly emerging TV market, but also for telephone traffic. The dramatic TV broadcast to the East Coast of President Truman's opening speech at the Peace Conference in San Fran-cisco was hailed as a technical marvel—for Bell.

Further, Bell battled hard so that it alone had the right to trans-mit such signals (Brock 1981: 183–184). Bell was not the only firm with the technology. Philco and Raytheon, among others, had de-veloped a wartime microwave capability and wished to serve this fast-growing market.[16] Indeed, the demand from the TV broadcast-ers outstripped Bell's ability to put microwave facilities in place, and early TV signals were carried on coaxial cable or even over private microwave systems that the FCC permitted to be built under ex-perimental license, only where Bell had no facilities. These private systems were limited in extent and, as Bell's network expanded, were gradually phased out. Bell argued before the FCC that it was putting in the facilities to do the job, it had the legal monopoly over common carriage of interstate electronic transmission, and it could use this profitable new service to offset the costs of the new facilities and keep rates to telephone users low.[17] The FCC agreed with Bell, and for more than twenty years Bell kept the TV transmission monopoly (FCC 1949b).

So what was the missed opportunity? Bell fought hard for the long-haul transmission of TV signals, which it saw as integral to its basic mission. What it missed was the truly profitable portion of the business: broadcasting. Bell possessed an almost unique technological advantage at a point when the radio networks were facing the substantial task of learning the new broadcast technology, with no access to intercity networking. Bell, having convinced the FCC that intercity signal transmission was exclusively theirs, could have gone on to argue adoption externality, just as it had argued universal service decades earlier, claiming that the only rational way to develop this new industry was as a single integrated enterprise, dedicated to the goal of getting a television in every home. By keeping the protection of regulation, under the rationale that Vail had used so successfully, Bell would have been in a position to extend its technological advantage in microwave transmission by forward integration into the profitable broadcasting (and TV set) business.

Pursuing such a strategy would not have been without cost. It may have forced AT&T to abrogate all or part of the 1926 cross-licensing agreement with GE, RCA, and Westinghouse, a pact that had served it well. However, GE's planned entry (with IBM) into data transmission via microwave in 1944 (Brock 1981: 182) indicated that GE was willing to put the agreement at risk for the sake of new markets, even if Bell were not. In addition, Bell would have had to argue, perhaps unsuccessfully, that the FCC should permit an expansion into nontraditional markets that could have attracted unwanted public scrutiny. We cannot know whether the potential profits of television would have warranted such aggressive actions, but the failure to consider entry into one of mid-century America's most profitable industries suggests a certain lack of astuteness regarding new market opportunities.

Today, it may seem almost inconceivable that the television industry could have developed in any other way. Yet in almost every other country in the world, television broadcasting was a state monopoly for the first twenty years, and today only a few countries have permitted private entry. Indeed, the U.S. model is almost unique in its reliance on private markets. In the late 1940s, it might not have been unreasonable for our nation's "state monopoly" for telephones, the Bell System, to make a bid to become our "state monopoly" for television.

Whether or not such a bid would ultimately have been successful is purely conjectural. But why didn't the Bell System even choose to try? Surely, the profit opportunities were evident. The radio networks and the set manufacturers certainly thought the profit potential large enough to take on the risks inherent in the adoption externality.

Bell's single-minded strategy of universal service (for telephones) caused it to be aggressive and tough when it saw opportunities to forward that cause (intercity TV transmission, for example, which could help offset costs of its telephone microwave network), but blinded it to new strategic thrusts. The exploitation of technology was vigorous and aggressive from the purely technical point of view, but curiously pedestrian from a market point of view.

Thus, Bell used this term of regulated monopoly to build and maintain an awesome technological capability, but a capability aimed at, and used for, its narrowly focused social/corporate goal of universal telephone service.

Should the share owners of record circa 1947 feel cheated? Perhaps not—these missed opportunities may best be viewed as part of the cost of the political compact that Bell had struck when it accommodated to regulation and the technological compact it struck with the 1926 cross-licensing agreement. When Bell bought regulatory and technological protection from competitive entry, the price may have been that Bell's business options were restricted to its then current markets.

From a social perspective, some may feel that preventing Bell from using its technology to expand its monopoly into other markets was an excellent idea. Had the Bell System become the nation's television monopoly in the late 1940s, the best we could expect is that it would be as good as, say, the BBC, Britain's television monopoly. Instead, television developed as an entry-controlled oligopoly, with three major network players, producing culturally dubious but enormously popular programming. Though obviously far from the economists' competitive ideal, only the most hardened aesthete would claim the superiority of the steady diet of Masterpiece Theatre and gardening shows of our British cousins over the wide range of nightly fare available domestically. Adopting even an imperfectly competitive market form has created a diversity and popular responsiveness in programming that has led TV shows to be an important U.S. export item.

The Strategy Endures: Market Developments

Missed opportunities were not the only way in which politics and technology affected markets. In 1930, the Bell System opened up the Pandora's box of sharing long-distance revenues with local operating companies, and the legacy has lived to haunt its heirs today. While this sharing, known as "separations and settlements," was initiated via the *Smith v. Illinois Bell Telephone Co.* case in 1930, its real roots are to be found in the politics of regulation and the focus of technological development at Bell Labs.

Recall that, historically, local operating telephone companies provided "exchange" service, consisting of (1) a telephone, generally in the customer's home or place of business; (2) an electrical connection between the phone and the company's local exchange switching office, called the "local loop" or the access line; (3) the service of interconnecting two customers within the exchange via the company's switching and transmission gear, called "local calling"; and (4) the service of interconnecting a customer with the long-distance network, so that the customer might call someone in another exchange area. AT&T, through its Long Lines division, provided the long-distance service—receiving, switching, and transmitting calls from one exchange area to another.[18]

Prior to 1930, each company had to set rates that covered the costs of providing its services, including the substantial capital costs associated with telephone plant. Local operating companies set rates for installing a phone, monthly service, and local calling. But during this period, most phone companies moved toward "free" local calls and installation fees substantially below the actual labor and capital costs of putting in a line and a phone. As a result, most of the local operating companies' costs were recovered through the monthly service charge, while AT&T recovered its costs through its per-minute rates for long-distance. The costs for the entire system were "assigned" to each company, and those costs were recovered in the company's regulated rates; the more costs you were "assigned" by the regulators, the higher your rates could be. All costs between the customer and the local company's switchboard were the local company's; all the costs between the local companies switchboards ("board-to-board") were AT&T's.

In Vail's day, providing local exchange service was relatively cheap and providing long-distance was relatively expensive. Transmitting a call across the country required the use of repeaters, echo suppressors, and other highly sophisticated (at the time) devices simply to make the distances. Until the 1950s, transmission remained the primary technical problem confronting Bell Labs' technical staff, and the resources of that organization were aimed at improving the quality and reducing the cost of long-distance transmission. At that time, however, the balance of costs reversed: transmission became very cheap, due to enormous technological advances, while local exchange had become expensive. The cause? The lowly access line, the local loop, still consisted of a pair of copper wires from the customer's telephone to the company's local exchange office, and in many cases it still needed to be installed by a skilled craftsperson. Wage inflation plus lack of any improvements in this technology ensured that the access line, and therefore exchange service, would gradually dominate the Bell System's costs.

This process was well underway in 1930, and eventually resulted in declining long-distance costs and rising local costs. In a more competitive industry, this changing cost structure would have been paralleled by a changing rate structure; in telecommunications, however, the goal was universal service, not competitive efficiency. Rising local rates could imperil that goal. If every telephone customer used the same amount of local and long-distance, reflecting the change in costs in the rates would have no equity effects, since the total bill would stay roughly the same for all. However, the distribution of long-distance usage across customers is quite skewed. Some businesses, for example, might use hundreds of hours a day, while some residential customers might never make a long-distance call in their lives. Hence, increasing local rates could deter some of these latter customers from getting a telephone, thus threatening universal service.

The political response to this impending threat came via *Smith v. Illinois*, and its logic was cast in terms of economic fairness. Any long-distance call, so the reasoning went, is a local call at either end. It uses the customer's telephone, the customer's access line, and the local operating company's switching and transmission plant.

Surely AT&T owes something to the local companies from the revenues it collects for these calls, as a sort of a rental charge for the use of these facilities. As a result of this decision, Bell, the independent companies, and the state and federal regulators established a system whereby a portion of local operating company costs was separated and assigned to interstate long-distance service, to be recovered in the per-minute charges AT&T levied for the service. AT&T would then settle with the operating companies by giving them an amount equal to these separated costs. Thus, the sharing of long-distance revenue with the local companies was implemented through this rather arcane "separations and settlements" process.

But wasn't all this just a charade? After all, the money was just being moved around among Bell companies—what real difference could it have made? As it turns out, it made, and continues to make, an enormous difference:

> Recall that most of the local operating companies were independents who had been saved by the Kingsbury Commitment from being gobbled up by Theodore Vail. Having been protected from acquisition and let into the long-distance network, they became junior partners in the industry, subscribing to the theory of universal service, but nevertheless adept at using their local political clout in the regulatory process. "Separations and settlements" meant, and means, money in their pockets—*Smith v. Illinois* represented a redistribution of income away from Bell and its customers and to the independents and their customers.
>
> Of course, the principal political reason for this revenue sharing was customer rates. Its net effect was to increase the amount paid by customers who were heavy users of long-distance and decrease the rates for local-only users. This sharing was thought to forward universal service.
>
> The economic effect was to decrease the monthly service charge and to increase long-distance rates, relative to costs, which would seem to violate the economist's principle that economic efficiency demands that price and cost be closely tied, with the result that such rates could cause efficiency losses.[19]
>
> Since the rates for long-distance were above costs, this practice certainly established incentives for potential competitors to

enter this newly profitable market. In order to maintain the Bell monopoly that supported these politically attractive rates, the regulatory barrier to entry was more essential than ever.

Yet again, we see technology and politics yielding a market solution substantially different from the competitive norm. The effect of technology on the costs of long-distance versus the costs of local prompted a countervailing political reaction that caused rates to tilt in the opposite direction. Potential profit opportunities were thus established in the service providing the subsidy (long-distance), which made the regulatory barriers to entry all the more crucial to maintain the system of subsidies under regulated monopoly. The motivation, of course, was universal service. Vail's shared social mission of a telephone for every household was still the Holy Grail of the Bell System and regulators alike.

In fact, by the late 1950s, this goal was coming close to reality. Following a very strong surge of demand for telephone service after World War II and the widespread use of automatic dialing, almost 80 percent of U.S. households had telephone sets within the home.[20] Universal service was in sight.

Notes

1. The path from invention to successful deployment of a new technology is often rocky. Overcoming the problems of implementing the simple concept of magnetic inductance coils involved a restructuring of engineering, manufacturing, and operations at AT&T (Wasserman 1985).
2. In fact, the actual mechanics of pricing and acquisition practiced by Bell were a good deal more complicated; this example serves merely to illustrate the principles.
3. If Bell had raised its local rates upon the introduction of long-distance, then Smalltown would only have to lower its rates to $3.00 below that of Bell.
4. Of course, Bell would not need to acquire Smalltown to realize the benefits of its strategy. It could offer to interconnect Smalltown with the long-distance network at a price that would capture all the value of that connection for Bell. During Vail's tenure, this approach was also used with the independents.
5. For an interesting account of the historical development of the uniquely American institution of regulation, see McCraw (1984).
6. In a 1913 agreement with the U.S. Attorney General, J. E. Kingsbury, vice-president of AT&T, committed to cease acquisitions of independent phone companies and to permit the remaining independents to interconnect with Bell's long-distance service. The Kingsbury Commitment ended for a time the

period of growth by acquisition; at this point, the Bell System owned 55 percent of telephones in the U.S., up from 49 percent in 1907.

7. Not only were these departments large, they were growing quickly. AT&T's annual report of 1913 states that 550 engineers and scientists were at work at headquarters. The 1920 annual report indicates that the technical work force had grown to 1,100, and, at the time Bell Labs was founded in 1925, 2,000 technical people were employed there.

8. Texas was the last state to adopt state regulation, following a scandal in the late 1960s.

9. For example, *Quick Action Collection Co. v. New York Tel. Co.*, P.U.R. 1920D 137 (N.J. Bd. Pub. Util. Comm'rs 1920) (DX 679), and *Pennsylvania Pub. Util. Comm'n v. Bell Tel. Co. of Pa.*, 20 Pa. P.U.C. 702 (Pa. Pub. Util. Comm'n. 1940) (DX725), among many others.

10. Shooshan (1984: Chapter 2) briefly summarizes the Walker investigation report and its aftermath, and outlines the issues in the 1949 antitrust suit.

11. In fact, deForrest had in mind radio applications for his 1907 invention of the audion; it was not until 1912 that either deForrest or Bell scientists considered applying the audion to long-distance telephone transmission.

12. Between 1930 and 1965, the cost per circuit-mile of long-distance transmission dropped by a factor of nearly ten (FCC 1966).

13. It can be argued that the public process of regulation tends to reward mistake-free performance (i.e., not attracting negative public scrutiny), but does not reward outstanding performance (Zajac, forthcoming). If cost reductions outstrip inflation, then a utility need not attract attention by asking for a rate increase (always unpopular and usually visible) and can often keep the difference as increased earnings. However, bringing new products to market is often viewed prospectively with indifference or even hostility by regulators and the public. Bell's efforts to introduce Picturephone service on a trial basis (probably ill advised) was greeted with derision by a New York Public Service Commission confronting a telephone service crisis: "Dial tone before Picturephone."

14. For example, Bell's commitment to put a phone in any home, regardless of its profitability. As a regulated common carrier, Bell companies were required to serve any household requesting service at the established and regulated rate. If the costs of providing the service exceeded the rate, it still had to be provided, in keeping with the universal service mandate. In a competitive industry, either the price to such customers would be increased to the point where it was profitable or they would not be served.

15. This concept is defined in Less (1984). Simply put, it only pays for firms to make, say, TV sets if other firms have already committed to produce ("adopted") programming, broadcasting, and intercity distribution. Of course, it only pays firms to commit to produce programming, broadcasting, or intercity distribution if other firms have already committed to produce and sell TV sets.

16. The principal non-Bell players in the video transmission via microwave sweepstakes were not signatories to the 1926 cross-licensing agreement. They were new entrants, who had gained their technical expertise under wartime conditions.

17. An AT&T witness stated Bell's case succinctly: "...the Bell System is in the best position to provide these nationwide television networks, and I think that will be in the best interest of the public to have the Bell system provide it [*sic*]. I think they can do it economically and do a satisfactory job as indicated in experience with program facilities and private line facilities and nationwide toll facilities" (FCC 1949a: 13).
18. While AT&T served all interstate long-distance, local operating companies did serve some intrastate long-distance. Which Bell system company served which intrastate long-distance markets, and which company owned or shared the facilities, seemed to be more a matter of historical accident than optimal system design. We focus our discussion on the interstate long-distance market, where the details of ownership are cleaner and do not obscure the economic and political principles involved.
19. But see the discussion of the network externality in Chapter 6.
20. 1986 household penetration is about 92 percent, according to the Bureau of the Census. Evidence by Perl (1985) suggests that market saturation has been reached.

References

Anderson, Douglas D. 1980. "State Regulation of Electric Utilities." In *The Politics of Regulation,* edited by James Q. Wilson. New York: Basic Books.

AT&T Annual Report. 1910.

Boettinger, H.M. 1983. *The Telephone Book.* New York: Stearn.

Bornholz, Robert, and David Evans. 1983. "The Early History of Competition in the Telephone Industry." In *Breaking Up Bell,* edited by David Evans. New York: North-Holland.

Brock, Gerald. 1981. *The Telecommunications Industry.* Cambridge, Mass.: Harvard University Press.

Communications Act, 47 U.S.C. para. 202(a) (1934).

Fagen, M.D., ed. 1975. *History of Engineering and Science in the Bell System: The Early Years.* Murray Hill, N.J.: Bell Telephone Laboratories.

———. 1978. *History of Engineering and Science in the Bell System: National Service in War and Peace.* Murray Hill, N.J.: Bell Telephone Laboratories.

FCC. *Telephone Investigation: Proposed Report.* Washington, D.C.: Government Printing Office (1938).

———. *In the Matter of American Telephone and Telegraph Co.,* Docket 16258, Bell Exhibit 24, Chart 4 (1968).

42 FCC 10 (1949a).

42 FCC 23 (1949b).

Goulden, Joseph. 1968. *Monopoly.* New York: G.P. Putnam's Sons.

Houk, Z.G. 1905. "Long Distance Telephone Lines." *The Telephone Magazine,* March.

Jackson, Charles. 1984. "Technology." In *Disconnecting Bell,* edited by Harry M. Shooshan, III. Elmsford, N.Y.: Pergamon Press.

Kernighan, Brian W. and Samuel P. Morgan. 1982. "The UNIX Operating System: A Model for Software Design." *Science* 215 (February 12).

Less, Nathaniel H. 1984. "Externalities, Information Costs, and Social Benefit-Cost Analysis for Economic Development—An Example from Telecommunications." *Economic Development and Cultural Change,* January: 255–276.

McCraw, Thomas. 1984. *Prophets of Regulation.* Cambridge, Mass.: Harvard University Press.

Paine, Albert. 1921. *In One Man's Life.* New York: Harper & Bros.

Perl, Lewis. 1985. "Social Welfare and Distributional Consequences of Cost-Based Telephone Pricing." Paper presented at the 13th Annual Telecommunications Policy Research Conference, Airlie House, Virginia, April.

Reich, Leonard S. 1977. "Research, Patents, and the Struggle to Control Radio: A Study of Big Business and the Uses of Industrial Research." *Business History Review,* 51.

Shooshan, Harry M., III, ed. 1984. *Disconnecting Bell.* Elmsford, N.Y.: Pergamon Press.

Smith v. Illinois Bell Telephone Co., 282 U.S. 133 (1930).

United States v. Western Electric Company, Inc., et al., Trade Cas. (CCH) para. 68, 246 (D.N.J.) (1956) ("Final Judgment").

Wasserman, N.H. 1985. *From Invention to Innovation.* Baltimore: Johns Hopkins University Press.

Zajac, E.E. Forthcoming. "Telecommunications: An Example of Policy Gone Awry?" In *Enterpreneurship and Innovation: The Impact of Deregulation on Airlines, Financial Markets, and Telecommunications,* edited by Gary Libecap. Greenwich, Conn.: JAI Press.

———. 1976. "Issues of Innovation and Technological Change." Paper presented at the Seminar on Competition in Regulated Industries, Eastern Illinois University, Charleston, Illinois, September.

CHAPTER 2

The Regulated Monopoly
Embattled: 1959–1974

More than the goal of universal service was in sight. As early as the late 1950s, small firms were emerging, eager to fill market niches in telecommunications. Philco and Raytheon's contesting of Bell's monopoly in the late 1940s for the carriage of TV signals on its microwave network indicates that at least some firms thought they could make a go of microwave technology. While they failed to carry the day, their efforts suggested that the capability and the markets were there.

Bell, however, had constructed a seemingly impenetrable double wall to protect its markets—the wall of superior technology and the wall of regulatory entry prohibition. Other firms may have had the technical capability to enter Bell's markets at this time, but the FCC's findings in the video transmission case suggest that the regulatory barrier was still firmly in place. Within a decade of that decision, however, the double wall of technology and regulation showed serious cracks. Within two decades, the double wall was in disrepair. Within three, it was almost completely demolished. The seismic tremors of technology and public policy were in motion; the constructed barriers of an earlier era could not withstand these fundamental forces.

Cruelly, it is sometimes our greatest successes that set the stage for later failure. The settlement of the Justice Department's antitrust suit against Bell in the 1956 Consent Decree was widely held to be an almost total victory for AT&T. Bell retained its structure, including Western Electric, and was "only" required to stay out of unregulated businesses and freely license its patents, including its basic transistor patents and the 8,600 patents covered under the cross-licensing agreements of 1926. This apparently small concession in fact made freely available all the technology for which

Bell Laboratories was so justly famous and permitted its use by other, newer firms, who would seek access to Bell's protected markets to exploit their new expertise.

Private Microwave: The First Crack

By the late 1950s, the cost of reliable microwave systems had reduced to the point where large geographically dispersed firms, which had tied their plants and offices together with Bell System communication lines, were considering purchasing and operating private microwave systems to carry their internal telephone traffic. Firms such as New York Central, which already owned its right-of-way, as well as organizations in airlines and trucking, were especially well positioned to take advantage of off-the-shelf microwave systems available from the likes of Collins Radio, whose systems operated at frequencies higher than Bell's standard TD-2 system. Bell opposed the use of private microwave systems by large corporate customers, seeking FCC protection from (self-) entry in this market niche. In the first of a series of cautiously procompetitive decisions, the FCC ruled against Bell in this case, *Above 890 MC*, permitting firms to own and operate systems for their own internal corporate uses (FCC 1959). This decision marks the beginning of the FCC's opening of Bell's markets to entry, but at the time it was not seen as consciously procompetitive (Hinchman 1981).

Although the *Above 890* decision involved only private communication systems, in no way interconnected to Bell's national network, Bell considered it a threat to Vail's "one system, universal service" policy and responded with full vigor. Bell asserted that the market was part of its "integrated system." Any entry would violate the system's integrity, and Bell could then no longer be responsible for any part of the system. "Harms to the network" could result; hence, entry needed to be forbidden. It also argued "economic harm." Since this market was alleged to be profitable, only Bell's monopoly position allowed it to keep basic monthly rates to consumers low, thus fostering universal service.[1] Bell attempted to brand competitive entry as "cream-skimming" lucrative markets, which would result in higher prices to telephone ratepayers.[2]

Having lost its case, Bell quickly devised an aggressively priced competitive tariff as a response to *Above 890*. The TELPAK tariff, offering deep discounts to users who could bundle 12, 24, 60, or

240 private line channels on a single route, was targeted at multi-location firms with large volume needs. This is the very highest end of the voice transmission market, consisting of a handful of firms generating a significant fraction of Bell's toll volume. When the TELPAK tariff was filed in 1959, it was intended to keep this market segment from switching to private microwave systems— and it did. Virtually none of the then planned private microwave systems were deployed. Competitors and others claimed that the price response was too aggressive, constituting not only price discrimination but cross-subsidy as well. Bell was pictured as temporarily willing to lose money in the subject market in order to drive its competition out of business and scare off future competitors[Bell's regulated monopoly markets were considered the funding source for Bell's anticompetitive pricing actions.]

This sequence of events was to become the pattern of regulatory dialogue in the coming years: a competitor seeks to enter some peripheral telecommunications market; Bell argues system integrity and economic harms to the telephone ratepayers; after losing, Bell implements a competitive tariff (or product); and finally the competitors and regulators charge Bell with cross-subsidizing competitive services from monopoly markets. Bell counters with the argument that price cutting in the newly competitive market helped them retain at least some of the profits from that market, thus contributing to the goal of universal service. Competitors and regulators continue to voice strong suspicions that Bell's price cuts are too deep and in fact result in predatory pricing via cross-subsidy.

The Cross-Subsidy Issue

An unintended victim of Bell's TELPAK tariff was Western Union, by 1960 already a shaky proposition. The concerns of Western Union, as well as the microwave manufacturers, were voiced before the FCC in demands for a cost study to determine whether or not Bell was using its monopoly services to cross-subsidize private line services via TELPAK.[3] These demands resulted in the FCC's request to Bell for a "Seven-Way Cost Study" to determine the rate of return for each of seven broad service categories within the FCC's interstate jurisdiction. The cost analysis was conducted under cost-allocation rules spelled out by the FCC, and the results corroborated the suspicions of the complaining parties—the rate of return on "MTT" (message toll telephone, or basic long-distance) was 10 percent, the rate of return on TELPAK was 0.3 percent, while the overall allowed (and realized) rate of return was 7.5 percent (Kahn 1970: 156–157). The FCC used the results of the study to justify launching the first comprehensive investigation since the 1930s into Bell's rate structure and ratemaking process (Docket 16258, announced on October 27, 1965). AT&T's stock price of $66⅞ quickly slid to under $60, and within months had fallen to $49¾. The three-month paper loss suffered by investors after the FCC announcement was $3.7 billion (Goulden 1968: 338).

Bell claimed that the method of allocating joint costs (inherently unallocable) to individual services could produce an appearance of cross-subsidy, given the huge joint and common costs of the telephone system. For example, if half of the firm's cost are joint, and if half of these costs were allocated to private line and half to MTT, then the rate of return to private line would look much lower than the rate of return to MTT. If only one-quarter of the joint costs were allocated to private line and three-quarters to MTT, the disparity would be less extreme. What proportion of joint cost should be allocated to each service? To almost all economists, any cost allocation is inherently arbitrary, so there can be no right answer—any such cross-subsidy calculation will be highly sensitive to the particular method of allocation. To prove the point, Bell cost analysts conducted the "Seven-Way Cost Study" using nine different methods of allocating costs, each equally plausible, and showed that the methods led to radically different answers. Their conclusion: what possible meaning could any of the numbers have if they depended so critically upon arbitrary assumptions?

Cross-subsidy, then, moved to the fore in the debate over competitive entry. If Bell reacted to a new entry with aggressive rate reductions, was this a truly competitive response (as Bell would claim) or a predatory response based on Bell's ability to cross-subsidize the competitive market with earnings in its monopoly market? It was believed that a regulated firm with access to monopoly markets would be more likely to engage in predatory pricing than would an unregulated firm, and so special regulatory watchfulness was in order. As long as Bell served both monopoly markets and competitive markets, Bell's competitors could always cry "foul!", claiming cross-subsidy and predatory pricing, unless the FCC had a clear, clean standard by which to judge whether Bell's rates involved such internal subsidies. As the Federal Communications Commission opened more markets to competitive entry in the 1960s and 1970s, the cross-subsidy debate became *the* central issue: how could the FCC control the potential abuse of Bell's market power in its monopoly markets to cross-subsidize its newly competitive markets with predatory intent?

Not that cross-subsidy was all bad. In the previous chapter, we described how separations and settlements provided for cash generated from long-distance calling to be used by operating companies to keep local-service rates low. However, "taxing" long-distance with the aim of enhancing universal service was "social" pricing, perceived to be a beneficial subsidy. If Bell were under-pricing its competitive services and overpricing its monopoly services in order to drive its competitors out of the market, this was clearly an abuse of its regulated status for private gain, and such subsidies were to be abhorred.

The *Above 890* decision, followed by Bell's aggressive TELPAK response and the competitors' subsequent demands that Bell's predatory rates be investigated, set the tone for the next two decades of telephone regulation: prevention of cross-subsidy by a firm operating in both monopoly and competitive markets.

Telephones and Terminals: Another Breach

Meanwhile, pressures for competitive entry in other markets were mounting. Among the various "foreign attachment" cases that Bell opposed over the years, the Carterfone case focused attention on the market for terminal equipment.[4] In 1965, Tom Carter, a Texas entrepreneur, filed an antitrust suit against Bell for threatening to suspend service to his customers who used his acoustically coupled device with their telephones (Brock 1981: 240). The suit resulted in a referral to the FCC. Bell opposed Carterfone before the FCC, on the grounds that Bell must control the entire system, out to and including the customer's instrument, in order to ensure proper functioning of all its parts. Bell claimed it was protecting the quality of service to all users from greedy entrepreneurs; others thought Bell was mainly interested in protecting the outer perimeter of its telecommunications system from encroachment by competitors.[5] Again, the decision eventually went against Bell, in the FCC's 1968

Carterfone decision (FCC 1968), but not before dozens of other firms entered the fray, wanting to sell telephone sets, data sets, key systems, and PBX's, all products directly competitive with Bell's offerings.

Although espousing open entry in the terminal equipment market, the FCC, recognizing the potential for as-yet-unproven harms to the network, asked Bell to file new tariffs with provisions to protect the network against harm. An obvious possible response would have been to specify in the tariff the technical standards that interconnecting equipment would have to meet in order to guard against harms to the network. Such a response would have been consistent with an earlier Supreme Court decision prohibiting IBM from insisting that only its tabulating cards could be used on its equipment, but permitting it to set standards for what kind of card could be used (*IBM v. U.S.* 1936). But Bell was decidedly unenthusiastic about the engineering-specifications approach for terminal equipment. Bell's position was that the network was far too complicated for simple standards to suffice, and that the FCC was incapable of administering a program of complex standards. Therefore, technical integration demanded that telephone sets be produced by the same entity that produced and operated the network: the Bell System.

AT&T's actual response to this new threat of competitive entry was much more aggressive. AT&T filed tariffs with the FCC specifying that non-Bell terminal equipment could only be connected to the Bell network through a Bell-supplied "connecting arrangement." Although a number of firms filed comments with the FCC that this tariff violated its findings in *Carterfone*, the FCC did not at the time agree, and it permitted the tariffs to go into effect.

Again, we see the same pattern that first emerged in the *Above 890* case: Bell first opposes opening the market to competition, the FCC permits such entry, Bell responds aggressively, and competitors complain that the response is unfair and anticompetitive. In the case of terminal gear, however, Bell's response seems particularly strong. By setting a high price for its connecting arrangement, Bell could make it economically unattractive for customers to purchase competitors' phones at any price. More likely, Bell could set the price high enough to extract any profits that new and innovative terminal gear might otherwise earn for new entrants. In effect, Bell sought to retain the ability to refuse interconnection selectively—*de facto*, if not *de jure*—by pricing. Of course, the regulators could disapprove a rate it deemed too high, but Bell's ability to play the regulatory game was substantial.

Bell's response to *Above 890* was a price cut aimed at those customers who would find private systems attractive; such customers gained by the tariff cuts, even if microwave manufacturers lost out. However, Bell's response to *Carterfone* had only one winner: Bell. Any new and innovative terminal product could succeed in the market only if AT&T got its cut of the profits, via its connecting device. Clearly, Bell had upped the ante in its competitive response. Rather than opting for interconnection by standard and decreasing terminal equipment prices to meet competition, Bell was able to maintain both its prices and its control of the market with its connecting arrangement tariffs. Still, some entry did occur—by 1974, new entrants had captured 3.7 percent of the market (FCC 1975).

Perhaps Bell's response to competitive entry in terminal equipment sprang from its realization that its own terminal products were not competitive. The lack of competitive terminal gear and plans to overcome this deficiency were discussed at the AT&T President's Conferences of 1970 through 1972 (Brock 1981: 243–244). Had Bell been prepared with products viable for a competitive marketplace, perhaps it would have adopted the less anticompetitive interconnection by standard. Regardless of the reason, Bell chose to tough it out.

Though the FCC had accepted Bell's tariffs, it apparently never bought into the connecting device idea. It continued to probe the need for such devices, carefully and slowly plodding through all of Bell's arguments regarding their necessity. Bell's position was that electrically attaching non-Bell telephone sets or PBX's to its network would cause harms ranging from improperly shielded sets sending surge voltages down the line and electrocuting telephone repairmen, to spurious signals injected into the network by these sets that might cause wrong numbers and incorrect billing to others. Such harms, it was claimed, could not necessarily be avoided by requiring that "foreign attachments" meet strict technical standards, since the institutions required to administer such a standards program were not in place.

Confronted with the doubts of Bell's technicians concerning the feasibility of the engineering standards approach, the FCC hit upon a brilliant tactic: ask the National Academy of Science to determine if such an approach could solve the alleged problem of harms to the network. The National Academy was august, learned, and could command the best resources of the scientific community. The FCC would be mustering one of the few effective counterweights to the enormous technical prestige of the Bell System. After another substantial delay, the NAS issued a report indicating that an engineering standards approach could successfully protect Bell's network from harms from other manufacturers' equipment, provided each design met stringent requirements. It also concluded, by the by, that the use of connecting devices was technically valid as well.

The FCC, pleased with the findings of the NAS, began a formal investigation in June 1972 to examine the possibilities of interconnection by technical standards. An FCC advisory committee issued suggested engineering specifications for terminal equipment to protect the network from harm. It proposed that all manufacturers of interconnect gear would be required to register their equipment with the FCC and aver that the equipment complied with whatever standards and specifications were agreed upon. Rather than addressing the feasibility of technical standards versus connecting devices, the proceeding actually became a negotiating forum for what those standards ought to be. By the time the FCC adopted the technical standards approach in 1975, Bell had managed to postpone real competition in terminal equipment for eight years and was to further delay its arrival in important PBX and key system markets for several more, through regulatory delays and impediments.

Long-Distance: The Heart of the System

In 1963, prior to the advent of terminal equipment competition, Bell was once again attacked in its private line market, this time by a young upstart company called Microwave Communications, Inc. (MCI), which wanted to offer private line services on a shared basis to business customers in selected cities. The *Above 890* decision had given individual firms the right to provide their own in-house systems of microwave communications, but not to resell or to share their systems with other firms. Therefore, only firms with telephone demand large enough to use economically an entire point-to-point microwave system could avail themselves of this new right.[6] However, if one firm was able to operate a system and resell pieces of its capacity to other firms, the economies of operating a fully loaded microwave system could be passed on to smaller firms who could not fill a system on their own or take advantage of the TELPAK tariff. It was this modification to the decision that MCI sought.

The market threatened by MCI's entry was substantially larger than that threatened by the *Above 890* decision, and Bell responded with vigor. It charged MCI with cream-skimming the most profitable heavily trafficked routes, which Bell used to support thinner rural routes through the process of rate averaging. MCI's entry, it was declared, would undermine this socially beneficial rate averaging, which helped bring telephone service to rural America. In its 1969 decision granting MCI the right to offer private-line services between Chicago and St. Louis, the FCC did not address these larger issues of cream-skimming and universal service, but rather chose to address only the facts of the particular MCI construction application for Chicago–St. Louis service (FCC 1969). After a number of regulatory delays, MCI received final authority in 1971 and opened its Chicago–St. Louis route for business the following January.

Others, however, did respond to the broader implications of MCI. A number of firms filed construction applications for microwave systems to provide services similar to MCI's. Again, Bell opposed these petitions and asked for delays of various kinds, alleging that the increased competition would lead to higher rates for customers, interfere with universal service, and attack the basic system of rate averaging. Nevertheless, in its 1971 *Specialized Common Carrier* decision, the FCC embraced a policy of open entry into the private line market by any firm.

While Bell waged regulatory war with equal vehemence against terminal equipment firms and long-distance private line firms, there seemed to be particularly strong feelings within the firm about the latter. MCI, especially, was able to develop a sympathetic public persona, casting itself in the role of David against Goliath, which the interconnect firms had never achieved. Most Bell employees, who perceived their role as one of public service, found this characterization offensive. In addition, Bell employees, oriented toward engineering and operations, tended to view the network as the heart of the business. Even though private line was electrically separated from the common user network, incursions into this area were definitely seen as a competitive thrust toward the heart of Bell's network. In contrast, terminal equipment was perceived as "peripheral," in the same sense that a computer engineer sees, and speaks of, a printer as a peripheral.[7] While the interconnect firms were seen as going for Bell's wallet, MCI was seen as going for the family jewels.

Against this background, it was no surprise that the battle over private line entry was particularly hard fought and vicious. Bell's responses to MCI and the specialized carriers were aggressive. First, Bell took full advantage of its abilities to impose delays via the regulatory process; thus, two-and-a-half years passed between the FCC's granting MCI a construction permit and the actual offering of service by MCI, of which actual construction took about seven months (Brock 1981: 213).

Second, Bell filed lower rates aimed at the specialized carriers' target market. In 1969, it filed its "Series 11,000" tariff, which lowered rates in areas of heavy private line demand. This was followed in 1973 by AT&T's "Hi-Lo" tariff, in which rates for private lines between high-density switching centers (generally in large metropolitan areas) were drastically lowered, while rates between low-density centers were somewhat increased. Of course, if Bell's arguments regarding cream-skimming were correct, this was a perfectly appropriate competitive response, *provided* that rates were not reduced below the marginal cost of the service.

Third, and perhaps most serious, Bell hotly contested the FCC's position that Bell had to provide interconnections between MCI and MCI's customers. Since MCI was in the long-distance business only, it required the use of local facilities to connect its customers to its long-distance network in each of the cities it served. MCI claimed that, as a common carrier, Bell should supply these facilities. In its *Specialized Common Carrier* decision, the FCC agreed.[8] However, Bell managed to postpone tariff provision of interconnection until 1974, and even these arrangements were unsatisfactory to the specialized carriers.

In keeping with the pattern of action/reaction established in *Above 890*, competitors complained bitterly of Bell's response, claiming it was predatory and based on Bell's ability to cross-subsidize losses in competitive markets with above-normal returns in monopoly markets. However, the markets opened by the *Specialized Common Carrier* decision were far larger than those opened by *Above 890*, so the stakes were much higher. Just as AT&T responded more strongly to the potential entry, so did competitors respond more strongly to the perceived predation by Bell. MCI used the events of this period to build its celebrated private antitrust suit against Bell. Both sides had again upped the ante.

The Strategy Unravels: What Happened?

Vail's strategy of regulated monopoly, based on technological dominance and the regulatory partnership, survived over fifty years (1907–1959) without a significant setback. In pursuing this strategy, Bell had confronted major challenges, such as the Walker Investigation and the video transmission battle, and won decisively. And yet, in the next fifteen years, Bell took several major hits that set Vail's strategy reeling. The magic of technology and the security of regulatory protection no longer seemed to insulate Bell's markets. The regulated monopoly was now facing competition.

Where did the magic go? Had Bell Labs' scientists become dumber? Was Bell's ability to deploy the technology that the Labs produced becoming less? Decidedly not; the 1940s and 1950s were in many ways a golden era of technology in the Bell system. Bell Labs' practically founded the field of solid-state physics at this time; the vaunted invention of the transistor, basis of the digital-electronics revolution, grew out of this effort. Similarly, the system was successfully deploying Direct Distance Dialing nationwide, as well as the sophisticated cable and radio transmission systems needed to carry the resulting telephone traffic. Technology was never better at Bell.

The problem was too much of a good thing. By the postwar period, the technology that Bell Labs created was diffusing to other engineers and other firms, helped along by its free availability under the 1956 Consent Decree. As Bell Labs scientists made transmission cheaper and better, they inadvertently made the technology more accessible. The very nature of scientific research also contributed to this diffusion. While specific devices can be patented, the theories upon which the devices are based cannot be, and Bell Labs had to be in the theory business as well as the device business. For example, the transistor could be (and was) patented;

the theory of solid state physics could not be patented, nor kept secret. Others could use the theory to make their own competitive advances to challenge Bell. Ironically, "these...breakthroughs were...the tools which would be used to dismantle the Bell System itself" (Boettinger 1983: 194).

But what about regulation? Both state and federal regulators had protected Bell against competitive incursions in the past—why the change of policy? Did they no longer believe that universal service was important? Again, the change in the regulatory climate can most likely be traced, not to Bell's failures, but to its success. By 1960, the shared social objective of universal service was close to being achieved. For fifty years, it had been the common touchstone of regulators and regulatees alike, and now it seemed to be in reach.

But if Bell had succeeded (or was about to succeed) in achieving universal service, then why was it necessary to continue to protect it from competitive incursions? If the logic of the Vail strategy was "Let us accomplish our goal of universal service without competitive interference," then that logic suggested that achieving the goal diminished the social need for regulatory prohibition of entry.

But more was going on than more technological diffusion and less regulatory willingness to exclude entrants. Potential competitors saw bigger profit possibilities than had previously existed. Since *Smith v. Illinois* in 1930, the difference between rates and costs in the long-distance market had been growing in order to help support local exchange service. To the potential competitor, this disparity between rates and costs meant one thing: profits. If an MCI were permitted to enter, it could provide the same service at a lower price, attract Bell's customers, and make a bundle. To Bell, the disparity between rates and costs represented a social subsidy to local exchange service, and the competitors were cream-skimmers, attracted only to the most lucrative markets and unwilling to commit to the goal of universal service.

During the years before 1959, few competitors could seriously challenge Bell's technological dominance, and those who could found regulators who weren't willing to let competitors distract Bell from its mission of achieving universal service. After 1959, more competitors had the technical wherewithal to challenge Bell in its markets, they had more reason to want to compete, and they found regulators willing to experiment cautiously with competition, now that universal service was within reach. In other words, pre-1959, few had the capability or the inclination to knock on the door, and the regulators had little reason to let them in. Post-1959, many could and did knock on the door, and the FCC had little reason to keep them out.

Most emphatically, Bell was not about to abandon its beliefs about the business it had literally created—service to the public, end-to-end responsibility, and system integrity. Bell saw itself battling the barbarians at the gates, in two of its most important markets: terminal equipment and private line. Clearly, the FCC had changed the ground rules, and, from Bell's point of view, seemed to be pursuing a deliberate policy of endangering the goal of universal service by breaking up the integrated network that had given this nation the world's best phone system. Within Bell, the problem moved to the very top of the corporate agenda: regulatory difficulties were interfering with the basic mission and fundamental strategy of the corporation. While there was optimism within the firm that reason would eventually prevail and the FCC would come to its senses, the gravity of the problem was recognized, and the counterstrategy well in place. As articulated by the chairman of AT&T, "...[Does] not [Bell] have an obligation—an unusual obligation—if you will—to take a stand in opposition to current trends and prepare [itself] to debate the issue explicitly, not only on the legal, legislative and regulatory fronts, but before the Court of opinion as well" (deButts 1973).

Notes

1. In *Above 890*, Bell claimed that permitting private microwave systems "...would cause irreparable harm to the telephone company's ability to provide a basic nationwide communication service...[and]...would not only increase the cost of communications to the Nation's economy as a whole but would cast an added burden upon the individual and the small businessman who would continue to rely on common carriers" (quoted in Waverman 1975: 388).
2. Bell's competitive disadvantage as the "supplier of last resort" was cited as a related "economic harm." As a public utility, it was required to provide sufficient facilities to handle all traffic, even at peak periods, thus ensuring underutilization of capacity in off-peak periods. This placed Bell at a cost disadvantage to competitors who were not required to maintain backup capacity (Faulhaber 1972; Faulhaber and Levinson 1981).

3. Western Union and Motorola complained to the FCC that the TELPAK tariff was discriminatory and merely a predatory pricing scheme (Brock 1981: 209–210).
4. That is, equipment used on the premises of a customer for originating and terminating telephone calls. Later terminology refers to this as Customer Premises Equipment, or CPE.
5. The *Above 890* decision, permitting private microwave systems, did not directly address the system-integrity issue, since such systems were not permitted to be connected to the public telephone network. Of course, the issue was raised indirectly, because there was no way for Bell to be sure that such connections were not being made without its knowledge through the customer's own switchboard or PBX. This became known as the "leaky switch" problem.
6. As noted above, Bell's TELPAK tariff dissuaded many firms that had been considering such a move, so few of these private systems were actually deployed.
7. Later, as Bell beefed up its marketing function to succeed in a competitive market, the marketeers viewed terminal equipment as the customer's sole tangible evidence of Bell's presence, and consequently of far greater marketing significance than network services, which were essentially invisible to the customer.
8. "...[E]stablished carriers with exchange facilities should, upon request, permit interconnection...[to]...the new carriers..." (FCC 1971).

References

Boettinger, H.M. 1983. *The Telephone Book*. New York: Stearn.

Brock, Gerald, 1981. *The Telecommunications Industry*. Cambridge, Mass.: Harvard University Press.

deButts, John (AT&T chairman). 1973. Speech presented to the National Association of Regulatory Utility Commissioners, September 20. Reprinted in *Heritage and Destiny*, by A. von Auw. New York: Praeger, 1983.

Faulhaber, Gerald R. 1972. "Competition and the Dynamics of Growth." Paper presented at the Dartmouth College Seminar on Problems of Regulation and Public Utilities, Hanover, New Hampshire, August.

Faulhaber, Gerald R., and Stephen B. Levinson. 1981. "Subsidy-Free Prices and Anonymous Equity." *American Economic Review* 71 (December): 1083–1091.

FCC. *In the Matter of Allocation of Frequencies in the Bands Above 890 MC*, Report and Order, 27 FCC 359 (1959).

FCC 13 2d, 434, 435 (1968).

FCC, *Radio Regulation*, 16 (1969).

FCC 29 2d, 870, 940 (1971).

FCC, Docket 20003, Bell Exhibit 20 (1975).

Goulden, Joseph. 1968. *Monopoly*. New York: G.P. Putnam's Sons.

Hinchman, Walter R. 1981. "Briefing Paper on the Evolution of Common Carrier Regulation." Paper presented to the Subcommittee on Telecommunication, Consumer Protection, and Finance of the House Energy and Commerce Committee, Washington, D.C., May 20.

IBM v. U.S., 298 U.S. 131 (1936).

Kahn, Alfred E. 1970. *The Economics of Regulation*. New York: John Wiley & Sons.

Smith v. Illinois Bell Telephone Co., 282 U.S. 133 (1930).

von Auw, A. 1983. *Heritage and Destiny*. New York: Praeger.

Waverman, Leonard. 1975. "The Regulation of Intercity Telecommunications." In *Promoting Competition in Regulated Markets*, edited by Almarin Phillips. Washington, D.C.: The Brookings Institution.

CHAPTER 3

The Regulators Embattled: 1959–1974

In the story thus far, regulators appeared in the early twentieth century as a new force to be reckoned with as Vail developed Bell's grand strategy for dealing with technology, public policy, and markets. In fact, how regulation developed reveals America's love/hate relationship with free-market capitalism. In order to understand the critical role of regulation in the continuing drama of telecommunications, it is necessary to take a side trip to explore its history.[1]

A Digression: History and Theory of Regulation (Revised)

Government regulation of private enterprise is indeed a uniquely American institution, a mechanism for dealing with industries that do not fit neatly into Adam Smith's marketplace version of Locke's Natural Liberty, which motivated the framers of our constitution. Regulation was seen as an institutional exception, a regrettably necessary intervention in the workings of the marketplace, which Smith said worked best when subject only to the invisible hand of competition. Even while establishing the legislature's right to regulate economic activity in *Munn v. Illinois* (1877), the dissenting Supreme Court justice, Stephen J. Field, expressed strong misgivings over granting such a right: "If this be sound law, if there be no protection either in the principles upon which our republican government is founded, or in the prohibitions of the Constitution against such invasion of private rights, all property and all business in the State are held at the mercy of a majority of its legislature."

It was only after the advent of the first truly large corporations—the railroads—that regulation came into its own. Influential contemporary observers doubted the ability of the competitive market to discipline these huge enterprises and championed the creation of "independent" commissions, endowed with the necessary expertise, to regulate and control the activities of these giants.[2] The first modern regulatory commission was the Massachusetts Board of Railroad Commissioners, created in 1869; the first federal board was the Interstate Commerce Commission, created in 1887 (McCraw 1984).

The increase in industrial concentration and the appearance of trusts in the late nineteenth and early twentieth centuries brought with them the Progressive Era, a political reaction to large corporations bound together by invisible financial ties that seemed beyond the grasp of the invisible hand. The Progressives sought to control this power through two mechanisms: antitrust legislation, and government regulation. As we saw in Chapter 1, these mechanisms were not independent; antitrust actions affected regulatory responses, and vice versa. In the case of regulation, the Progressive agenda was clear: independent expert commissions would control industries in which competition did not seem to work, thus ensuring that the public interest, not just private interests, would be served. The regulatory commission was the Progressives' bulwark against monopoly power.

The intellectual heritage of the Progressive Era was adapted to the needs of Depression America by the New Deal reformers of the Roosevelt administration. The nation then faced an apparent breakdown of the market economy on a worldwide scale, which had thrown millions out of work and stripped away the legitimacy of the competitive marketplace. Since the market had failed so miserably to meet the economic needs of Americans, surely the government had to step in. The regulatory commission was an important vehicle for this intervention. In fact, the extant federal commissions today mostly date from either the late nineteenth and early twentieth centuries (ICC, FTC) or the depression era (FCC, CAB, SEC).[3]

All of these commissions had strong powers over the industries they regulated, including the power to approve or disapprove rates, capital investment, and entry and exit into specific markets by new firms and by incumbent firms. And all of these commissions were enjoined by their enabling statutes to regulate their industries to promote the public interest.

However, no clear definitions of "public interest" were ordinarily given to commissions. They were relatively free to interpret their social objectives, and history has shown that different commissions at different times had rather different views of the public interest. Clearly, the Progressives saw the regulators as controlling the monopoly power of the regulatee to bring lower prices, and nondiscriminatory prices, to consumers. In the case of the Food and Drug Administration, regulators were to ensure consumers of safe, unadulterated food and medicine. In later years, Brandeis and others saw regulators as ensuring that competition among firms was not *too* fierce, which would lead smaller firms to go under—"big is bad" was the watchword, even if consumers had to pay more for it (McCraw 1984: 101–109). As issues of income distribution gained in political importance, many regulators saw achieving income redistribution through utility rates as a legitimate public interest concern.

One interpretation of public interest that has been used by economists derived from the idea that regulation was to act as a surrogate for competition in industries where competition was not feasible. The philosophical underpinning of Adam Smith's version of "Natural Liberty," that is, the competitive market, was the maximization of "the wealth of nations" by encouraging the most efficient use of society's scarce economic resources. In industries in which competition did not lead to the maximum efficient use of resources, then regulation should attempt to correct this deficiency. The proper role of the regulator was to foster economic efficiency: the efficient level of investment, the efficient operation of the business, and the efficient allocation of the monopoly's output to consumers by means of prices. Of course, this view could be at variance with an approach to the public interest based on income redistribution, preserving small firms in the market, or protecting existing firms from "instability".[4]

In the 1950s and 1960s, this conception of public utility regulation came under attack by economists and political scientists. The economists' attacks at first focused on the actual economic performance of regulation (for example, MacAvoy 1965), noting large discrepancies between actual use of resources and efficient use of resources. The attacks of the political scientists focused on the naiveté of those who expected the regulatory process somehow to be free of politics, suggesting political models of regulatory behavior. Bernstein's lifecycle theory (1955) suggested that regulatory agencies started with fervor and youthful vigor, but eventually fell under the influence of those they regulated and settled into spine-less senility, serving the industry they were supposed to control.

Economists and political scientists became very active in the 1970s, developing theories of regulation. The earlier public-interest theory (and indeed Bernstein's lifecycle theory) were discredited, as scholars refined their ideas and tested them against available data. Stigler (1971), for example, put forward a "producer-protec-tion" theory of regulation, in which the actual (as opposed to the publicly announced) rationale for regulation was to achieve greater profits for the regulated. Thus, the establishment of the ICC in 1887 was viewed, not as a means to control the railroads' profits and prices for consumers, but rather as a cartel manager for the railroads themselves, maintaining high rates and punishing those that attempted to "cheat" by lowering prices. This is also consis-tent with Kolko's explicitly Marxist argument (1965).

Posner (1974) suggested that parties other than producers could strongly influence regulators as they seek to cross-subsidize their particular interest groups through a regulated firm's rates. Regu-lation, then, could be seen as imposing taxes and subsidies to ben-efit some at the expense of others. The work of political scientists on the behavior of legislators (Mayhew 1974; Fiorina 1977) is con-sistent with this point of view, and various empirical studies con-firm it (Ferejohn 1974; Scher 1960). Peltzman (1976) discussed the supply side of regulation: what was in it for regulators? He noted that there will be "demanders" of regulation (those demanding a subsidy, or demanding protection from competition, or seeking electoral visibility and credibility by demanding "protection" for others) and "suppliers" of regulation (legislators and bureaucrats who exercise the power of the state to compel), who provide regu-latory vehicles for demanders in exchange for money, power, po-litical support, media exposure, or other coin of the political realm.

The economic theory of regulation was wholly inconsistent with the public-interest theory: Regulators were not dispassionate ex-perts controlling the behavior of monopolies in the name of public interest, but, rather, were self-interested parties—like any other actor in the economists' worldview—seeking political and perhaps economic gain from their positions by way of political support, favorable media coverage, larger agency budgets, and perhaps a chance at higher elective office.[5] Petitioners and other parties with an economic interest in regulation also pursue their own interests by providing the resources regulators and politicians need in return for regulations favorable to them. In this theory, regulation is best analyzed from the perspective of who benefits, and who pays.

Wilson (1980: Chapter 10) presents a political scientist's model, wholly consistent with the economists' theory of regulation, that focuses on the technology of political influence and control. Following the economists, Wilson suggests that the degree of concentration of winners and losers is critical to both the format and the outcome of regulation. He considers all four possibilities: whether the beneficiaries are highly concentrated (electric power) or widely dispersed (environmental), and whether those that pay are concentrated (auto safety) or dispersed (protective tariffs). He also notes the recent rise of the political entrepreneur, whose use of the media can galvanize otherwise dispersed and unorganized people into an effective interest group (Ralph Nader, Howard Jarvis).

The economists' theory of regulation bears a striking resemblance to their theory of markets in a laissez-faire economy—there are demanders and suppliers, a technology of political influence, and political entrepreneurs. Since economists, particularly of the Chicago persuasion, sing the praises of the competitive market for goods and services, can we deduce that they likewise think highly of a market for regulatory influence?

In fact, quite the opposite is true. The economists' critique of regulation, if true, is damning.[6] In the economists' stylized market for goods and services, the competitive interplay of self-interested parties leads to an efficient allocation of society's scarce resources only because all exchanges are voluntary. Consequently, only mutually beneficial transactions actually occur, and it is through this myriad of voluntary exchanges that the invisible hand moves the economy toward the most efficient use of resources. By contrast, the market for regulatory favor is precisely the opposite of a voluntary exchange; it is a market for the coercive power of the state. When a favored interest group convinces a regulator to protect it from competition, that protection hurts others not party to the transaction—potential competitors who are thus excluded from the profits of the market and consumers who would otherwise benefit from lower prices and more variety. It is the very nature of regulation to compel economic agents to *involuntary* exchange, or to nonexchange: Potential competitors are prohibited from entry, utilities are required to serve favored customers at below-cost prices, consumers are required to purchase service from the franchised monopoly.

But enough of theory. We know that the economists' stylized competitive marketplace almost never occurs in practice. The truth is, every firm in the economy struggles to find that product or service that will distinguish it from its competitors, that will give it the ability to charge more than cost, that will enable it to escape from the tyranny of competitive forces long enough to make a few extra bucks. But every firm knows that in the long run, be it a few days or a few years, its competitors will match or even surpass it, prices will be bid down toward costs, and the struggle must begin again. The forces of the competitive market do not guarantee perfect efficiency at all times; far from it. But under certain conditions, market forces will *tend* toward efficient use of resources, eventually wiping out pockets of monopoly profit or poor performance. The system is far from perfect and at any particular moment in time may seem to be rife with inequities. Its redeeming value is that it generally exerts constant and unrelenting pressure toward efficiency.

Regulatory control, however, exerts constant and unrelenting pressure toward inefficiency. Firms that perform poorly, such as certain airlines prior to deregulation or electric utilities overcommitted to nuclear power, are not permitted to fail, but are bailed out by their regulators, either through arranged merger or increased rates to consumers. Innovations that could upset existing market structures are blocked from the industry (Kahn 1970: 165). Uneconomic subsidies enter the rate structure and usually increase. Without the self-correcting aspects of the market, the inefficiencies of regulation tend to multiply.

Owen and Brauetigam (1978) emphasize the growing importance of (indeed, obsession with) procedure in the regulatory process. They refer to the "judicialization" of regulation, wherein the observance of due process for all parties slows down decisionmaking to a snail's pace. Change is extremely difficult, thus implicitly acknowledging parties' rights to the status quo. This may reflect the aversion of most people to the risks of an economy subject to oil shocks that increase (or decrease) the price of gasoline, technical innovations that may wipe out jobs, or demand shifts that favor, say, small cars over large ones. While these changes are inevitable in a dynamic, responsive economy, they can often be disruptive to groups of consumers, employees, and firms. If they can be slowed or even stopped by recourse to the political process, then many will demand that regulation favor the status quo, according to Owen and Brauetigam.

It has long been recognized by economists that even in the best of circumstances, market forces work imperfectly in urging the economy toward efficiency, and there are many (well-understood) circumstances in which we simply cannot count on the market to effect its discipline. What we are now seeing is that the American alternative, regulation, may perform even more poorly. Neither institution is perfect, but the incentives for inefficiency built into the regulatory process, as well as the lack of corrective forces, should make us extremely cautious about relying on regulation to improve matters for consumers. Nor can matters be improved by finding better regulators or by better crafting enabling legislation. The inherent flaws are in the process, not the people. Only in very rare circumstances have individual regulators worked against the natural tendency toward more control and less efficiency.[7] Exceptions aside, it appears that the cure (regulation) may be far worse than the disease (market failure).

This thumbnail sketch of the economic theory of regulation may appear unduly harsh toward the regulatory process—surely it can't be all that bad! The evidence from the airline industry, the only example of truly complete deregulation, suggests that, yes, it really *is* that bad: gross inefficiencies in operations and system design, poor pricing practices, and substantial underutilization of capacity were all substantially reversed after deregulation. According to Bailey, Graham, and Kaplan (1985: 196), "Deregulation has shown that the well-intentioned and orderly views of the regulators caused enormous distortions in productivity and in service." Even though the airline industry may be far from the economists' ideal competitive market, the performance of even this imperfect version in the first five years after deregulation outstripped the economic performance of the industry under regulation. Of course, lessons drawn from deregulation in one industry should not be applied without wisdom to another, but we ignore them at our peril.

The Theory Applied: Bell's Regulatory Compact

In view of the modern theories of regulation discussed above, Vail's regulatory strategy seems especially astute. Vail's policy of immediate accommodation ensured that Bell was the only "interested party" close to, indeed in partnership with, the regulator.[8] By announcing a common goal, universal service, Bell gave the regulator the political justification to brush aside potential competitors, barring their entry into the regulatory game. Only two players were involved: Bell and the regulators. They often scrapped over who would get how much, but they seldom argued over who was to sit at the table. Over the years, Bell's regulatory compact with the commissions was broadened to include key parties: rate averaging greatly benefited rural and small-town customers at small cost to urban customers; separations benefited local residential users at the expense of toll and business users; settlements benefited the independents in return for political support for the system as a whole. Just as Bell sought to deny others access to its markets, it sought to deny access to the regulatory game. In fact, the nature of regulation demanded that it do so to maintain its monopoly market position.

Bell's ability to exploit the regulatory process was impressive. As we mentioned in Chapter 2, MCI was prevented from starting operation of its private-line service between Chicago and St. Louis until 1972, nine years after it first petitioned for access, although actual construction of the system took only seven months. MCI claimed it spent $10 million on regulatory and legal fees, and less than $2 million on the facilities themselves (Brock 1981: 213). And over seventeen years passed from the introduction of Carterfone until customers could legally purchase and use telephones of their choice, without financial obligation to Bell.

This is not to say that Bell's use of the regulatory process to produce long delays was intended to deny benefits to the public for its own private gain. Many people within Bell strongly believed that these competitive incursions were as bad for the public as they were for AT&T. However, the regulatory process allowed them to translate that belief into a successful delay strategy that would not otherwise have been possible. Few today would doubt that, at least in the terminal equipment market, delay imposed substantial losses on potential suppliers and potential customers alike.

Before we can understand why this regulatory compact unraveled, we first need to be explicit about what the compact was and who got what out of it. What the regulators got was:

Prices below historical costs for monthly service, which encouraged customers to join the telecommunications system;

Prices below historical costs for all services to rural customers,
who would otherwise face high rates;
Steady technological innovation, which caused the real price
of telephone service to drop steadily through the 1960s; and
High-quality, reliable service.

Keeping prices below costs benefited the many at the expense of
the few, which helped regulators maximize votes at the expense
of efficiency. Reliability and steadily dropping prices ensured that
regulators need not justify unpleasant changes to irate telephone
users, as they later had to do in the 1970s. This is not to say that
consumers did not push for lower rates for themselves and a lower
rate of return on Bell's capital (pressures Bell strenuously coun-
tered). However, during this period, the regulators had no problem for which the answer was more competition.

What Bell got was:

Complete protection from competitive entry in all markets;
Ability to control the rate of technological innovation, thus protecting the value of current assets;
A return on capital and a growth rate that made AT&T the glam-
our stock of the postwar era.

In the face of decreasing nominal costs of telephone services in
the 1950s and 1960s, Bell could actually lower its prices and still
have steadily growing earnings. Its heavy investment in Bell Laboratories was safe, since innovations developed internally could
be deployed in a fashion that protected current asset values. Further, the technical leadership of Bell Labs seemed to guarantee that
few other firms would ever have the technology to challenge Bell
in its primary markets.

From the regulators' perspective, the reasons for protecting
Bell were strong—the rate structure that promoted universal service (e.g., rate averaging) could also attract entry, since low-cost
areas and markets subsidized high-cost areas and markets. Hence,
limiting entry encouraged the enormous postwar growth of the
telephone industry, reaching out to rural America without the necessity of government financing.[9] Likewise, the reasons against
protecting Bell were very weak—after all, who was being kept
out? Bell's technology was so strong that few firms were up to
the challenge, so the regulators hardly ever had to say no. Occa-
sional challenges, such as the Philco and Raytheon attempts in

the 1940s, were easily turned aside, a small price to pay for universal service.

The Compact Unravels

The strength of the argument to protect Bell came from the shared social goal of universal service, and by 1960 that goal had largely been achieved. When the objective first enunciated by Vail fifty years before was in hand, the sense of a shared mission and common goals that underlay the regulatory compact slipped away. From the regulators' point of view, Bell looked less and less like a dedicated public servant working hard to put a telephone in every home and more and more like a high-growth fat cat anxious to exploit its unique market position. With universal service in place, the need to protect Bell from competition became much less obvious.

On the other hand, what was the harm of protection if Bell's dominant technology and seemingly unchallengeable control of the field meant that few firms could take Bell on anyway? However, the presence of an increasing number of firms on the regulator's doorstep, looking to enter, strongly suggested that Bell's technology was no longer so advanced, hence its costs so low, that rate averaging and other subsidies would not attract entry. Others saw profit opportunities from their knowledge of the technology and the price/cost disparities that regulation had induced. The list of reasons that the regulators could plausibly give for denying them the right to compete was short. In a nation whose political economy is based on the benefits of the competitive market, protecting the world's largest firm from its discipline is not politically feasible in the long run.

Of course, such fundamental changes in social direction seldom announce themselves. At no time did the FCC explicitly consider whether a ban on entry in telecommunications continued to be necessary after universal service had been realized. Nor did the regulators note the growing variety of electronic gadgetry available to consumers and firms and express an interest in making this equally available in telephonic form. Rather, the political will to maintain a partnership dedicated to the populist vision of a telephone in every home naturally dissipated once the goal was achieved.

However, the economic theory of regulation suggests that the truly revolutionary effect of opening the door to competition was not market entry into previously monopoly markets; it was increasing the number and kind of players in the regulatory game. The FCC's competitive experiments did more than establish token competitors; they changed forevermore the structure of the game. Once MCI or the interconnect manufacturers were in the market, they had a real, visible stake in regulatory outcomes and would seek to influence the regulators toward actions favorable to them and unfavorable to Bell. Further, their ability to influence regulators was much greater as an operating incumbent than as a hopeful outsider. As instruments of the FCC's new policy, the new entrants knew the commission had a stake in their survival. They could expect—and they received—regulatory treatment that ensured their financial health.

The modern theory of regulation gives us insight into the apparently excessively strong positions that Bell adopted regarding essentially trivial market issues. For example, the *Hush-A-Phone* case (1956) involved the proposed sale of a plastic mouthpiece extension that gave the caller more privacy from others in the same room who might overhear that end of the conversation. Bell did not itself offer such a device, nor did it propose to; it simply wished to establish a precedent that *nothing* that it didn't sell or lease could be connected in any way to its system. The facts of the case did not seem to warrant Bell's heavy-handed approach, and, although the FCC originally found for Bell, its ruling was overturned a year later. It's likely that such tactics weakened Bell's overall public credibility.

Bell's point of view, however, was based on the "camel's nose in the tent" theory: Once even the smallest portion of the camel is permitted in the tent, eventually the entire camel will end up inside. Bell's regulatory strategists thus saw their job as smacking noses, no matter how small or seemingly innocuous. Bell engaged each case of actual or potential entry and each case of foreign attachments, no matter how small, backed by the full weight of its corporate legal staff.[10] Regulatory theory suggests Bell's strategists had it right; subsequent events confirmed this: Not only is the camel in what Bell perceived to be its tent, but the previous occupants have been evicted.

None of this made the FCC's job any easier. Not only were more and more firms requesting the right to sell their wares in some lucrative telephone market, but Bell was treating each case as a life-or-death issue, insisting on arguing all the issues in protracted proceedings. While Bell no doubt thought this strategy would cut down the number of potential competitors by sheer economic attrition, it certainly made life painful for the FCC and its staff.

The FCC's Economists

This FCC staff played a vital role in the unfolding regulatory drama. In the early to mid-1960s, the FCC retained a number of young economists, whose procompetitive, anti–big business view was shared by other regulatory economists who came to professional maturity in New Deal and post–New Deal America. Economists such as Manley Irwin and Bill Melody vigorously upheld an image of Bell quite at variance with the picture of "your friendly telephone company".[11] According to them, bigness tends to breed abuses, and, since the Bell System was the biggest of all, it was guilty of the greatest abuses. The cure was to encourage new firms to enter telecommunications, protecting them if necessary against predation by Bell. This view is strongly reminiscent of Louis Brandeis's battles against bigness in the first half of this century (McCraw 1984: 101–109), even in its support of government protection for the small producer at the expense of higher prices to consumers. For the first time, the FCC was hearing from economists on its staff, and the message was strong, clear, and different from the prevailing wisdom: more competition, and don't trust Bell.

The FCC's actions during this period were much more cautious than the rhetoric of the young economists would suggest. Nevertheless, the intellectual position that competition should be encouraged took root. In effect, the staff itself became an important player in the regulatory game, a role that would grow in importance in the coming years. While many of these economists had left the FCC by the early 1970s, and a new generation of economists took over, the positive view of competition and the negative view of Bell had become ingrained in the FCC staff.

The Datran Caper

During the early 1970s, the FCC and the new entrants were becoming as adept as Bell at playing the regulatory game. As we'll see in the next chapter, they learned to play it so well that they were soon besting the old champ. But the rituals and rhetoric of the game were so complex and obscure that only an expert could tell what was going on, as illustrated by the brief career of Datran, Inc.

Founded as a subsidiary of University Computing Corporation, Datran was one of the many firms that applied to the FCC after the MCI decision for permits to build microwave systems. Its target, however, was the emerging business-data market. Datran claimed that it would fill a need for digital technology in this market that Bell was not able or willing to satisfy. Unlike MCI, Datran also maintained that a technical wrinkle, digital transmission, would allow it to carry high-speed data traffic more efficiently and accurately than the older analog facilities of Bell.

At this time, the FCC was struggling with the issue of permitting open entry in the private-line market. Clearly, the commission wished to extend the very limited authority it had given MCI to encompass all potential competitors, but it was concerned about Bell's strong opposition, based on the claim that such entry would take away business that Bell had been using to support universal service. As Owen and Brauetigam (1978) point out, regulation often gives incumbents a de facto "right" to their existing markets, and this is exactly what the FCC did, not wishing to appear to be letting the potential new entrants steal Bell's market.

Datran's petition was therefore a godsend to the FCC. In its *Specialized Common Carrier* decision in 1971, the FCC permitted open entry, but only by those, such as MCI, Datran, and others, who would be offering new, heretofore unrealized services through previously unavailable technology. It asserted that such entry would encourage "innovative" services, which might actually benefit Bell by adding new markets, rather than simply diverting existing business. The underlying technology of MCI, Datran, and others was microwave, then entering its third decade of faithful service to the telecommunications industry. Only Datran had actually proposed an innovative system (digital radio) aimed at a new market (high-speed data). Most of the parties understood that the basis of the FCC finding was a polite fiction. Nevertheless, it provided a rationale, which could not be proved wrong in a court of law, for the *Specialized Common Carrier* decision permitting entry by non-Bell firms into the private line market. The term "specialized" even suggested that such firms would indeed be highly specialized, serving markets that Bell had largely ignored. Of course, to no one's surprise, such was not the case.

While Datran had served the FCC's ends, it did not fare well in the market. It quickly built its digital radio network and was in operation by 1973. However, Bell introduced the DUV tariff as a competitive response to the Datran digital-radio threat. DUV stood for "Data Under Voice"—Bell Labs engineers had discovered that a small change in the tuning of the ubiquitous TD-2 FM radio (microwave) system made available a radio spectrum "under" (i.e., at a lower frequency) the main voice-carrier frequency. This spectrum was particularly suitable for digital signals. Therefore, Bell could offer a digital radio service piggybacked on the TD-2 system at very low cost (aside from the opportunity costs of spectrum). In keeping with the pattern of action/reaction established during and after the *Above 890* decision, Bell contended that its knowledge of the technology permitted this competitive response to Datran. Consequently, it filed the tariff in 1974, Datran claimed predation, and the FCC ordered an investigation, while the new AT&T rates went into effect. In 1976, the tariff was declared unjustified and predatory, but was permitted to remain in effect under appeal. Before the full commission could rule on the appeal, Datran went bankrupt.

The regulatory rhetoric engaged in by both sides often led to tortuous reasoning. For example, in opposing entry, Bell typically argued that the market in question was already well served by them, needing no competitors to improve the lot of customers. When Bell filed selectively lower rates after entry occurred, this could not be termed a response to competitive entry since that would suggest that Bell had needed the spur of competition to undertake rate action favorable to customers. Bell had to maintain that its competitive responses (e.g., the discovery of the DUV capability of the TD-2 system) were not responses at all, just business as usual. On the other side of the market, the specialized carriers had their own fictions. MCI and Datran both lobbied the FCC hard to keep Bell's rates high, to make their own offerings more attractive. Of course, the business customers that MCI and Datran were attempting to attract were also large purchasers of Bell services, and the specialized carriers' lobbying activities worked against the interest of their clients. These carriers had to strike a delicate balance between wooing corporate clients who would benefit from lower Bell rates and vehemently opposing any such lowering of rates at the FCC.

The Bell Economists

One important consequence of the FCC's efforts in this period, although unintended, was the vastly increased use of economists to help shed light on the issues. As economists were put on the FCC staff, the nature of the debate underwent subtle changes. Witnesses for the staff concerning the proper rate of return to be allowed on AT&T's interstate investment were now academic financial economists, such as Myron Gordon and Harold Wein, who used models of financial markets and regression analyses to support their recommendations. AT&T continued to use J.J. Scanlon, its treasurer of many years, whose testimony, based on extensive experience, carried great weight, but couldn't negate the opinions of the academics. Professional journal articles, such as Averch & Johnson's 1962 *American Economic Review* article on the incentives of a rate-base-regulated firm to use capital inefficiently, were introduced by academic witnesses on behalf of the staff.

Although it was not clear what effect this new group of witnesses was having, Bell apparently found this attack from a new quarter somewhat unnerving. As the presence of economists in the regulatory process increased during the late 1960s, Bell switched its response from one of ridicule to one of accommodation. It retained leading American economists, William Baumol, Alfred Kahn, and Otto Eckstein, as advisors and witnesses. In 1970, it funded a new professional journal, the *Bell Journal of Economics and Management Science* ("*and Management Science*" was later dropped), devoted to the study of problems in industrial organization and regulation, which quickly became the top industrial organization journal in the world. And it established a Management Sciences Division at AT&T to examine and analyze mathematical and empirical approaches to regulation. Meanwhile, several groups at Bell Labs became interested in such problems. For example, AT&T called upon its eminent Bell Laboratories' statistician, John Tukey, to help refute Professor Myron Gordon's 1966 rate-of-return testimony before the FCC.

Eventually, a group of research economists was established at Bell Labs, focused on a broad array of problems associated with regulation and other issues in industrial organization. During the 1970s, this group made significant contributions to these fields, earning a name consistent with Bell Labs' overall reputation for research excellence. The recognition afforded these researchers by other economists, including those at the FCC, on congressional staffs, and in other policy positions, gave AT&T a regulatory edge, but one it never felt comfortable using. Even though its researchers had "captured the high ground" of the economic theory of regulation, AT&T regulatory strategists never lost their sense of economists as outsiders who didn't appreciate the Bell System and were in large part responsible for the attacks on it. This sense is forcefully expressed by Alvin von Auw[12] (1983: 131–132):

...not even among its own most intimate economic counselors could AT&T generate...enthusiasm for opposing competition.... Differ as they might on particulars...AT&T's economists and those of its opposition shared a common philosophy—...the economists' view of the way the world ought to work. ...[one of] AT&T's original "board of economic advisors"...Alfred Kahn, of course, was the Carter administration's arch deregulator and shows no sign of repentance. Ironically, he was abetted in his deregulation of the airlines by his deputy at the CAB, Elizabeth Bailey, formerly of Bell Laboratories.

We may suppose that only Mrs. Bailey's gender spared her the sobriquet "henchman" in favor of the term "deputy" above, in light of Mr. von Auw's deep feelings about economists and his penchant for turgid prose.

Whatever else can be said about the drawn-out regulatory process of the 1960s and 1970s, the contributions of economists to the field of regulation were considerable. These advances have already had significant impact on the regulatory analyses of other industries, such as airlines and railroads, even more so than in telecommunications.[13]

On the Cusp of Change

The Bell System entered the mid-1970s sobered by its failure at the FCC to stem the tide of competition. While it had been successful in delaying and delimiting competition, it had not blunted the FCC's broad thrust toward more open entry. It had seen the ability of the new entrants to play the regulatory game increase substantially. Furthermore, Bell had used up considerable credibility in defending its positions. Its allegations concerning "harms to the network" were deemed especially shaky, since those harms seemed to exist only in the minds of its engineers. Bell Laboratories' reputation for scientific objectivity suffered the more its scientists contributed to the "harms to the network" story. Bell's defense of its position had been strong, but its prospects for the future were cloudy.

Bell's competitors, on the other hand, could be cautiously optimistic. MCI, Sprint, and the interconnect manufacturers had at last been dealt a hand in the regulatory game. The success of the FCC's procompetitive policies was dependent in part on the business success of the new entrants, so they could correctly anticipate favorable decisions. Further, the new entrants had developed considerable expertise at the game, most of it from their experience at the hands of Bell. In the coming years, they would show that they were better at it than their mentor.

The FCC entered the mid-1970s with some successes but with more question marks. Its *Specialized Common Carrier* decision had not resulted in much entry and had really annoyed Bell. Further, what entry had occurred apparently was being overpowered by Bell, and the dispute never seemed to get off the regulatory docket and fully into the marketplace. The terminal equipment registration decision was approaching, after ten years of delay and obfuscation, and would be another test of competition; if it failed, the FCC would be a very visible goat for the American public. The FCC's procompetitive policies had been implemented very cautiously and very slowly. Bell had had time to mount its full defenses, and the regulatory process had to grind them down.[14] If the FCC was procompetitive, it surely was not precipitously so.

Notes

1. This very brief sketch of the theory of regulation does scant justice to a rich research literature in several disciplines. A contemporary source for a more complete outline is Noll (1985).
2. Hadley (1886) saw the oil, steel, and coal industries, "which involve large capital under concentrated management," as inherently monopolistic, rendering "the old theory of free competition...as untenable as it was in the case of railroads."
3. We focus here on price and entry regulation of specific industries, not on regulation of activities, such as job safety (OSHA) and environmental quality (EPA), which date from the decade of 1965–1975.
4. A more comprehensive review of the objectives and performance of regulation is given in Schmalensee (1979).
5. A regulatory commission might appear to be a poor place to start a political career, since the position seldom warrants anything other than negative

attention. It should be recalled, however, that one of the twentieth century's most popular and flamboyant politicians, Huey P. Long, began his public career as a Louisiana railroad commissioner.

6. This is not to say that all, or even most, economists find these criticisms compelling. Such astute observers as Alfred Kahn and Stephen Breyer (1982) see a continuing need for regulation, albeit regulation safeguarded from "cartelization and anticompetitive protectionism" (Kahn 1983: 27).

7. Alfred Kahn at the CAB leaps quickly to mind as everyone's favorite candidate (McCraw 1984). Elizabeth Bailey, Kahn's colleague at the CAB, and Darius Gaskins of the ICC are also deserving of special mention.

8. For our purposes, references to "the regulators" will mean the FCC, unless otherwise specified. In fact, telecommunications regulation is conducted at both the federal and the state level; state public utility commissions control prices, quality, investment, and entry of telecommunications firms solely within their state boundaries. Monthly rates for local service, rates to install a telephone, what type of phones may be leased or sold, and toll rates to call within a state are approved by the state PUC. The Federal Communications Commission regulates prices, quality, investment, and entry on all interstate matters, including interstate toll rates, interstate WATS rates, private line rates, and in recent years rates for terminal equipment used for interstate services. On certain matters of mutual interest, such as separations and settlements, federal and state commissioners will constitute a joint board. During the period of the policy debate ending with the announcement of divestiture in 1982, the state regulatory commissions played a very limited role, no doubt being occupied with the rampant inflation of the time, as well as public concerns over nuclear-power generators, which issue was also within their jurisdiction.

9. Although the Rural Electrification Administration, designed to electrify rural America, also found itself making low-interest loans to small independent telephone companies.

10. This policy had been in effect since the time of Vail and had been largely successful, especially at the state level.

11. The view of these economists was also at variance with later proponents of deregulation and competitive markets, whose focus is efficiency and product innovation.

12. Mr. von Auw was AT&T vice-president and assistant to the chairman from 1969 to 1981.

13. See, for example, Bailey's foreword to Baumol, Panzar, and Willig (1982), which contains a neat bit of intellectual history regarding the research processes of economists at Bell Laboratories.

14. As compared to the CAB's deregulation of the airlines, in which the Board acted far more quickly than either the firms or the courts could handle.

References

Averch, Harvey, and Leland L. Johnson. 1962. "Behavior of the Firm under Regulatory Constraint." *American Economic Review* 52 (December): 1052–69.

Bailey, E.E., D.R. Graham, and D.P. Kaplan. 1985. *Deregulating the Airlines.* Cambridge, Mass.: MIT Press.

Baumol, W.J., J.C. Panzar, and R.D. Willig. 1982. *Contestable Markets and the Theory of Industry Structure.* New York: Harcourt Brace Jovanovich.

Bernstein, M.H. 1955. *Regulating Business by Independent Commission.* Princeton, N.J.: Princeton University Press.

Breyer, S. 1982. *Regulation and Its Reform.* Cambridge, Mass.: Harvard University Press.

Brock, Gerald. 1981. *The Telecommunications Industry.* Cambridge, Mass.: Harvard University Press.

Ferejohn, J.A. 1974. *Pork Barrel Politics: Rivers and Harbors Legislation.* Palo Alto, Calif.: Stanford University Press.

Fiorina, M.P. 1977. *Congress: Keystone of the Washington Establishment.* New Haven, Conn.: Yale University Press.

Hadley, A.T. 1886. "Private Monopolies and Public Rights." *Quarterly Journal of Economics* 1 (October): 28–44.

Hush-A-Phone Corp. v. U.S. and FCC, 238 F. 2d (1956).

Kahn, Alfred E. 1970. *The Economics of Regulation.* Vol. 1. New York: John Wiley & Sons.

———. 1983. "The Passing of the Public Utility Concept." In *Telecommunications Regulation Today and Tomorrow,* edited by Eli M. Noam. New York: Law & Business, Inc.

Kolko, Gabriel. 1965. *Railroads and Regulation, 1877–1916.* New York: W.W. Norton.

MacAvoy, P.W. 1965. *The Economic Effects of Regulation.* Cambridge, Mass.: MIT Press.

McCraw, Thomas. 1984. *Prophets of Regulation.* Cambridge, Mass.: Harvard University Press.

Mayhew, D.R. 1974. *Congress: The Electoral Connection.* New Haven, Conn.: Yale University Press.

Munn v. Ill., 94 U.S. 113, 140 (1877).

Noll, R.G. 1985. "Government Regulatory Behavior: A Multidisciplinary Survey and Synthesis." In *Regulatory Policy and the Social Sciences,* edited by R.G. Noll, pp. 9–63. Berkeley: University of California Press.

Owen, B.M., and Ronald Brauetigam. 1978. *The Regulation Game.* Cambridge, Mass.: Ballinger.

Peltzman, S. 1976. "Toward a More General Theory of Regulation." *Journal of Law and Economics* 14 (October): 109.

Posner, R. 1974. "Theories of Economic Regulation." *Bell Journal of Economics and Management Science* 5 (Fall): 335.

Scher, S. 1960. "Congressonal Committee Members as Independent Agency Overseers: A Case Study." *American Political Science Review* 54: 911–920.

Schmalensee, Richard. 1979. *The Control of Natural Monopoly.* Lexington, Mass.: D.C. Heath and Co.

Stigler, G. 1971. "The Theory of Economic Regulation." *The Bell Journal of Economics and Management Science* 2 (Spring): 3.

von Auw, A. 1983. *Heritage and Destiny.* New York: Praeger.

Wilson, James Q., ed. 1980. *The Politics of Regulation.* New York: Basic Books.

CHAPTER 4

The Policy Debate
Engaged: 1974–1981

The mid-1970s saw a very substantial increase in the pace of the policy debate on telecommunications, as well as a substantial increase in the number of players in the game. By the end of the decade, virtually all branches of the federal government were taking an active role in the debate, and yet events had quite gotten out of the FCC's (or anyone's) hands. The rather stately pace of change that characterized the 1960s and early 1970s accelerated to a sprint during the latter half of the decade.

New Initiatives

The Registration Program: Serious Competition

By 1975, the FCC's registration program for simple customer premises equipment (CPE) went into effect; within six months, the FCC had extended it to include all CPE, including PBX's, coin phones, main stations, and key systems. Several court challenges stayed the order until October 1977, when it became effective.

Competitors, both foreign and domestic, targeted all market segments, from home customers interested in owning their own phones or wanting additional features such as built-in memory, to small, medium, and large businesses with PBX's and key systems. Almost immediately, Bell's loss of market share increased, but not in all market segments. Large firms, which relied on Bell's PBX's and the after-market service and support it could provide, stayed with Bell, while other large firms with their own communications managers opted to choose their own PBX's. Telecommunications consultancies sprang up to help customers through the maze of new products and new firms. Small to medium-sized firms, who had never had the level of service and support that Bell afforded to the larger firms, were seduced by the attention they were getting from the new competitors, and Bell's market share of the key-system market steadily dropped. Home customers tended to stay with Bell, though "pioneer" consumers readily switched to the new products.

For the regulators, though, the message was clear: allowing competition increases consumers' choices, brings new products into the market, and generally makes everyone except Bell happier. Further, beyond losing business they thought was theirs, Bell could not demonstrate that any of the "harms to the network" they had predicted came to pass. Competition in terminal equipment, now called customer premises equipment (CPE), was an unqualified success. The appetite of policymakers at the federal level was whetted for further competitive entry.

The Machineries of Justice

Others were dealing themselves a hand in the Washington telecommunications game. After several years of preparation by its Antitrust Division, the Department of Justice filed a major antitrust suit against the Bell System in 1974, in which it alleged numerous conduct violations. There was every indication that this was a major suit, which would take years, perhaps decades, to resolve, that would require extraordinary defense measures on the part of Bell. The discovery process alone would take at least three to five years.

Justice's bold move encouraged private parties to turn to the antitrust court. By 1979, forty-nine private antitrust suits had been filed against Bell (Brock 1981: 295). At least some of these complainants hoped to free-ride on evidence turned up by Justice in its case and possibly even to gain summary judgments if Justice won. The combination of treble damages, the deep pockets of Bell, and free evidence from the Justice case was tempting to many firms.

A New Initiative from Bell

Faced with reverses at the FCC and this new and very serious challenge from Justice, public affairs issues rose to the absolute top of the AT&T chairman's agenda. Although the sailing had been rough for the past decade, Bell now saw hurricane-force winds gathering on the horizon. The public-policy debate threatened to get out of hand, and Bell's business future was at risk.

John deButts, AT&T's chairman in the mid-1970s, came to AT&T by way of Illinois Bell. His time in the Federal Relations Department had prepared him to defend aggressively the corporate and social objectives that had made the Bell System great and in which he believed: universal service and regulated monopoly. Unfortunately, his stewardship of AT&T occurred at a time when his skills were not a good match for the broad policy problems it faced. His performance in maintaining earnings during a period of inflation was by any measure excellent; had his ability to deal with the public policy problems affecting the future of the industry been as impressive, his tenure would be cited with more honor than it is. History recalls John deButts as the man who dug in his heels, who would not compromise, who would not give an inch. No doubt his response to the multiplying challenges to his company's mission came from deep inside, from the values inculcated over an entire Bell System career. This was not a man who could violate his values or defend them with less than his full energies.

As an activist executive, deButts had difficulty dealing with the ambiguities of the evolving policy debate, seeking instead to slice through this Gordian knot with a brilliant coup that would free Bell from the frustrations in which it was enmeshed. Consequently, he asked AT&T's public affairs and legal people to draft a bill, to be submitted by friendly congressmen, to cast in legislative concrete the concepts and values that had guided communications regulators and executives alike for sixty years. The Consumer Communications Reform Act (CCRA), intended to replace the Communications Act of 1934 as it applied to telephony, proposed to make regulated monopoly, low rates for monthly service, subsidies to rural areas, universal service, and no competition the law of the land, thus reversing the decade-long policy drift at the federal level toward competition. CCRA was introduced by a number of congressmen in 1976, with more sponsors being added with each passing week. Initially, it looked as if the strategy just might work. As the session wore on, however, it became clear that quick action would not occur. The bill was referred to the House Subcommittee on Communications, chaired by Congressman Van Deerlin of California.

The deButts legislative strategy represented both the strengths and the weaknesses of Bell's public policy planning. Bell saw itself being dragged down, sapped, by Washington bureaucrats and self-styled experts who sought to ram "reform" through the administrative process. Surely the American people would be outraged if they knew that their friendly Ma Bell was in jeopardy. Therefore, they went to the house of the people, the U.S. Congress. Surely the grassroots strength of all those telephone employees on school boards and town councils, running Little League teams and mobile blood donor trucks, would persuade Congress to find a way out of this insanity.

But AT&T found that customers were cool toward the Bell version of events. A survey conducted by Bell in Illinois in the early 1970s suggested that Bell's view of competition as anticonsumer and anti-universal service was not shared by the very consumers whose cause Bell thought itself to be championing. An AT&T report (1974) summarized the results of this survey:

...the actions we protest against (e.g., certifications; proposals to open our markets to competition) are seen as reasonable solutions to problems or as ultimately beneficial to [Bell].... If the public is to adopt our position fully it must...suspend its convictions and accept the antithesis of some long-held beliefs (e.g., that "free enterprise" means higher prices and lower product or service performance; that the government, in the body of the FCC, would deliberately take actions harmful to the public interest...).

Bell's use of the survey results is instructive. Rather than adapting their corporate strategy to conform to what the public seemed to believe, Bell sought to change the public's beliefs, to convince them that Bell's view was the right one. To that end, in 1974 Bell organized its "Impact" program, sending out "...Bell System spokespersons by the hundreds, each one equipped with a script, a set of charts and a discussion leader's guide...to alert their neighbors to the fact that already decisions had been made in the public's name...[the consequences of which]...they would not like" (von Auw 1983: 90).

Who can guess what the true impact was of this earnest band of Telephonians, flip-charts in hand, issuing apocalyptic warnings. What we do know is that the practical impact of "Impact" was zero. When Bell went to Congress, it had absolutely no grassroots support for its proposals. In spite of its vast resources and its long-standing Washington presence, Bell's political muscle was amazingly flabby.

But Bell had got their attention. Now the telecommunications was on the congressional agenda, the House was determined to do something about it. In 1978, Van Deerlin's staff produced draft legislation (H.R. 1978), reworking the entire Communications Act of 1934, including not only telephone, but TV and radio as well. The initiative was now with Congress, not with Bell, and Congress was beginning to be in a procompetitive, antiregulation mood. Senator Kennedy had already started hearings on airline deregulation, and by 1978 Congress would move decisively on that issue. Van Deerlin's draft legislation announced a legislative goal of competition wherever possible, clearly not a bill to Bell's liking.

DeButts' attempt to slice through the Gordian knot turned out to be just another punch at the tar baby. Not only had this stroke failed to clear up the regulatory mess or the antitrust mess, it had added a new legislative mess. The brave offensive quickly turned out to have opened a new front where Bell had to throw even more resources to help avert disaster. Bell was thus fighting a three-front war and losing on all of them.

Congress did not act on the new proposal (in fact, it never got out of committee), primarily because all affected parties found something in it to dislike intensely. Van Deerlin left at the end of the session, vowing to consider the bill again in the next. After two tries and two failures (H.R. 3333 in 1979 and H.R. 6121 in 1979–80) just to get a bill reported out of committee, Van Deerlin's constituents turned him out of office, and the chairmanship fell to Congressman Tim Wirth, an aggressive young politician from Colorado. A more savvy player than Van Deerlin, Wirth kept the issue alive and tried to build various coalitions, none of which included Bell and none of which seemed to be able to win. The successive legislative drafts, however, began to take on a tone that was rather ominous for Bell; not only were they highly procompetitive, in the sense of allowing new entry, they also became progressively stricter in their proposals to prevent Bell from cross-subsidizing and driving out competitors. Bell was the one player in the game that needed to be restrained, that could not be permitted to play by the same rules as the new competitors. In fact, the presence of competitors was seen as requiring even greater vigilance and tighter controls on Bell by regulators. Although these congressional debates did not lead to legislation, they set the tone and pace of policy considerations both for the FCC and in antitrust court.

What had happened to raise this specter? By the mid- and late 1970s, the issue was no longer whether competition would be permitted, but rather how much and how quickly competition should be let in. The success of competition in CPE was an accomplished fact; now, how could other markets be opened up?

By 1978, the great policy question was "How can we assure that Bell will not abuse its monopoly position in some markets to throttle new entrants in competitive markets?" The FCC and Congress listened sympathetically to the new competitors' tales of cross-subsidy, predation, and denial of access by Bell. Policymakers had watched Bell's aggressive responses to entry following *Above 890, MCI, Specialized Common Carrier,* and *Carterfone.* The conflicting claims of Bell (legitimate competitive responses) and its competitors (predatory) could not be easily resolved, but procompetitive regulators and legislators were willing to err on the side of the new entrants by handicapping Bell's ability to respond. The new competitors, now able players of the regulatory game, pressed for even greater controls. On its part, Bell claimed that it, too, wanted to compete but insisted on a "level playing field," with no handicaps.

Both Congress and the FCC agreed on the overriding policy issue of the late 1970s. Despite enormous huffing and puffing, the policy machinery of the U.S. government, including the FCC, the Justice Department, the District Court, and the U.S. Congress, failed to solve the problem.

The Control of Cross-Subsidy

The Accountants' Solution

Strenuous attempts to resolve the issue were made. A 1975 solution was to have Bell develop an extraordinarily detailed cost manual, so that each expenditure for labor or capital for AT&T's interstate service would be assigned to a specific service, such as WATS or private line, and even to an individual price element, such as evening rates for long-distance calls over 1800 miles. This solution sought to resolve by brute force the dilemma of the allocation of joint costs raised in the "Seven-Way Cost Study" of 1964 (see Chapter 2, pages 25ff): any joint costs would be assigned to the services in proportion to the forecasted use of the joint facility. When Bell asked for a specific rate increase, it would be expected to compare the proposed rate to the allocated cost associated with that rate element, to determine whether or not prices matched costs. Should there be a deviation, Bell would be expected to prove that it was justifiable on grounds other than cross-subsidization. This approach would, in effect, ensure that Bell could not make *any* response, competitive or predatory, to entry by new firms, since the demand for proof would be extremely difficult to meet. As it had for its *Specialized Common Carrier* decision, the FCC made up a story, which, if true, might have merited this regulatory accounting, but was recognized as false by almost all parties except its proponents— namely, that the costs so calculated by the cost manual allocation approach approximated economic costs, on a "cost-causative" basis.

In general, this type of price-formula regulation—"price equals cost"—is attractive to regulators because it appears to be a fair and simple approach to ratemaking. The Interstate Commerce Commission used such a formula to regulate surface transportation rates, and the CAB implemented a price formula in the early 1970s in its Domestic Passenger Fare Investigation. However, the joint and common cost allocation problem in telecommunications ensured that all the action was then concentrated on the method by which costs were allocated. Since the allocation method determined the price structure, debates among Bell and its competitors before the FCC would now be about cost allocations, not about rates.

Somewhat later, the FCC announced it would completely overhaul the Uniform System of Accounts (USOA), to update and modernize it so that it could be used to detect cross-subsidy and help in rate decisions. How this effort was to fit with the cost manual work underway at the commission and at Bell was unclear, but the USOA docket was started with high hopes of solving the primary regulatory dilemma of the decade: control of cross-subsidy.

The Structuralist Solution

In 1979, Charles Ferris, procompetitive chairman of the FCC, appointed Phil Verveer, a young Washington lawyer, chief of the Common Carrier Bureau, to complement other procompetitive staff changes.[1] Verveer had been lead counsel for the Department of

Justice in preparing the AT&T case. He soon steered FCC policy away from cost accounting as an instrument of social policy, toward a greater reliance on market forces to control Bell's market power. Cost accounting moved off center stage of the policy drama.[2]

Instead, Verveer sought to introduce certain *structural* modifications that promised to use Bell's own profit incentives, rather than strict regulatory oversight or accounting, to prevent predatory cross-subsidy. The structural approach was first broached in the Commission's findings in its *Second Computer Inquiry* (CI-2), an FCC inquiry into the appropriate boundaries between the highly competitive computer industry and the regulated monopoly communications industry. The *First Computer Inquiry* (CI-1) had ended in 1970 with the finding that telephone companies would not be permitted to enter markets involving the processing (as opposed to the transmission) of electronic signals, except through a fully separated, arm's length subsidiary. Since Bell had agreed not to enter into any unregulated market under the terms of the 1956 consent decree, CI-1 simply defined what the computer business was; the separate subsidiary clause had no significance.

The *Second Computer Inquiry* findings of 1980 changed all that. It okayed Bell's entry into any market as long as such competitive activities were isolated within a fully separated subsidiary (FSS), which would still be subject to nominal oversight by the FCC. Bell would still be formally regulated, thus satisfying the 1956 consent-decree terms, and yet would not be subject to price and entry/exit regulation. The only hitch: the FSS must deal with the regulated monopoly portion of the business at an arm's length basis; anything made available to the FSS must be made available to all on the same terms and conditions. Any attempt to subsidize the FSS would result in subsidizing all its competitors. For example, if Bell attempted to cross-subsidize its forays into the competitive CPE market by selling PBX's produced by Western Electric below cost to its FSS marketing arm, then any competitor could also purchase the same PBX's from Western at the very same price. Since the FSS would be separated from Western (and the rest of AT&T), the price and terms of the PBX transaction would be public and visible, so others could claim the same benefit. Under such conditions, an attempt by Bell to engage in cross-subsidy across the FSS boundary would be completely ineffective and wasteful. In other words, CI-2 sought to use Bell's own market incentives to make cross-subsidization unattractive. Shortly after the FCC's initial findings, Bell indicated it would set up such a subsidiary and transfer all people and assets associated with competitive services and products to it.

While reaction was mixed, it was also quite strong. Senator Harrison Schmitt and Congressman Tim Wirth, both active in pending legislation, roundly criticized the FCC for attempting to resolve the issue without them, which the FCC denied.[3] However, Congressman Van Deerlin said the FCC "hit a home run." The interconnect manufacturers were certainly upset, since an unregulated Bell could eventually be a formidable competitor, even though the period since the FCC's registration decision had shown Bell to be particularly slow footed in CPE competition.[4] Many policy analysts and observers noted that it was almost impossible to have a truly arm's-length relationship and still be in the same firm; there would always be some way to beat whatever system the FCC set up, at least in theory. The FSS might receive the benefits of Bell Labs' research, paid for by monopoly revenues, or the FSS could receive a special marketing boost if it advertised jointly with its monopoly corporate partners. Therefore, competitors objected to any scheme that allowed Bell some competitive freedom.

Nevertheless, CI-2 moved ahead, although the restrictions placed on dealings between the FSS (promptly named "Baby Bell" by the press) and Bell became progressively stricter. Bell had responded to CI-2 as a man overboard might respond to a life preserver: he might have been hoping for a cruise ship, but he would settle for anything that kept him afloat. CI-2 looked like the best thing to come out of Washington for a long time. In spite of the heated criticism, Verveer and the FCC had come up with a winner in CI-2.

A Stake in the Heart of the System

For all the talk of competition and the opening of markets, Bell had managed to limit the incursions of competitors to what it saw as the periphery of its business: CPE and private line. In the case of CPE, we noted in Chapter 2 how Bell engineers saw such equipment as peripheral. While Bell clearly wanted to keep the CPE business to itself, losing that battle really affected only the outer perimeter of the system. Likewise, a private line sold to a Bell customer used a dedicated (to that customer) transmission facility and was not integrated into the common-user shared network that constituted the heart of what Bell believed to be its core business. The enemy had penetrated the outer defenses, but Bell still controlled the switched network.

But not for long. In 1973, MCI filed a tariff for Execunet, a service by which MCI's customers could dial a number in a distant city served by MCI and be connected to that number over MCI's "private lines," even though that customer had not leased a private line from MCI. With Execunet, an MCI customer need not actually lease a line from its home city to another location. The line could be "leased" just for the duration of the call. In this way, MCI sought to have customers share its private lines, making it a switched common-user network, rather than a collection of dedicated private-line facilities. In short, Execunet was nearly identical to regular, everyday long-distance telephone service. AT&T saw immediately that Execunet was equivalent to MTS (Message Telephone Service, formerly MTT), its mainstream market. If MCI were permitted to use its facilities in this manner, all of Bell's long-distance revenues, not just the 10 percent from private lines, were at risk. In 1975, Bell complained to the FCC, which directed MCI to stop, pointing out they had exceeded the authority of the *Specialized Common Carrier* decision, which explicitly permitted only private-line competition. MCI now found itself in the position of an incumbent with an existing service up and running. It appealed the commission's decision on procedural grounds, using the same tactics that Bell had used so successfully to maintain a valued service even over FCC objections. After nearly a year, however, the commission found against MCI. MCI again appealed, and in 1977 the D.C. Appeals court reversed the FCC on the grounds that "specialized common carriage" had not been adequately defined, that the Communications Act of 1934 had not granted AT&T a monopoly over long-distance and, in any case, could not do so without evidence that such a monopoly was in the public interest. MCI was therefore free to offer Execunet unless and until the FCC made such a finding.

The court's finding was upheld by the Supreme Court, but Bell announced that it would not supply the needed local facilities to connect MCI's customers to the new service, since the FCC's previous orders regarding interconnection via local distribution applied only to private-line services. The FCC supported AT&T's position, but MCI went back to the D.C. court, and again the FCC ruling was reversed.[5] By 1978 Execunet was in the clear; despite opposition by both Bell and the FCC, MCI now had a stake in the long-distance business. Bell agreed: a stake had been driven into the heart of the system.

MCI wasted no time exploiting its victory, soon offering its switched service to residential as well as business customers, primarily to fill its facilities in the off-peak evening. Its market now tremendously expanded, MCI underwent a period of 100 percent annual growth for several years, as it capitalized on this new opportunity.

The Structuralists Strike Again: Resale and Arbitrage

MCI still faced tough competition from Bell's interstate WATS (Wide Area Telephone Service), introduced in the mid-1960s, by which a firm could lease a WATS line from its place of business to the local switch, over which a call to anywhere in the country (or selected successively contiguous regions) could be made. The WATS line cost a fixed amount per month, with a marginal price of zero per call. This service was targeted at firms with large calling volumes not concentrated among a few points (for which private line was the cheaper alternative). MCI's pricing and market segmentation placed it head to head with Bell's WATS service, and WATS was very attractive. The specialized carriers thus saw WATS as their most difficult competitor.

WATS also bothered the FCC, and for years the WATS tariff was left in place as "unlawful, but not illegal," that is, the FCC didn't know if it was discriminatory or not, certainly didn't want to bless the tariff in any way, but did not want to infuriate the many WATS customers by forcing withdrawal of the tariff. The basic question: WATS seems to be plain old long-distance service, packaged for the large user — why is it priced differently? The commission's suspicion was that WATS was simply a form of market segmentation and price discrimination and should therefore be illegal. They framed the question, "is WATS 'like' or 'unlike' MTS," and initiated an inquiry into the issue in the mid-1970s.

Verveer and the FCC staff made the WATS issue the second major thrust (after CI-2) toward structural solutions to solve the cross-subsidy dilemma. For years, the commission couldn't decide whether or not WATS was "cost justified," nor could it decide whether it was an MTS clone. Verveer and Co. approached the problem from an incentives perspective, forcing Bell to remove the restriction against resale in the WATS tariff. If WATS were simply a market-segmentation pricing mechanism, then long-distance carriers could buy a WATS line and resell the service as an MTS look-alike to retail customers. Resale of WATS would thus permit the arbitrage of Bell's rate schedule for switched long-distance service. However, if WATS were something other than a volume-discounted MTS, then arbitrage would not occur. If substantial arbitrage did occur, it would be in Bell's interest to reduce the gap between MTS and WATS prices, simply as a competitive response to resellers. In doing so, of course, Bell would be reducing the degree of price discrimination between MTS and WATS.

The FCC, faced with deciding whether WATS was discriminatory, and, if so, what to do about it, turned the question from an administrative into a market issue. No need to weigh evidence, hear conflicting stories from interested parties, wade through massive cost studies, and finally bring the issue to an inconclusive end after several years. In the new structuralist regime, the commission could find the pressure point—the WATS resale restriction—fix it, and let the market work out the solution, trusting Bell's keen instincts for survival to eliminate profit opportunities its prior price discrimination had opened up. Accordingly, the FCC ordered Bell to remove all resale restrictions in its tariffs for MTS and WATS. Bell was permitted to file new WATS rates prior to the removal of the restrictions, and it did so on June 1, 1981.

The economics of WATS resale were straightforward. An outgoing WATS line cost a customer approximately $3000 per month[6]; if the customer could keep the line busy eight hours per day with long-distance calls, then the average cost per minute would be about $0.20. The corresponding average cost for long-distance MTS was about $0.33. Consequently, a reseller could rent a storefront in any town, buy some WATS lines, a small PBX switch, and local exchange service from the Bell operating company, and go into business reselling WATS. The resellers' customers could simply call a number, dial in their ID number, be connected to the WATS line, and reach their party. The reseller could charge, say, $0.28 per minute, thereby undercutting Bell's MTS service by 15 percent.

The reseller's WATS costs would be $0.20 per minute, and other costs (office rent, purchase of a PBX, customer billing, etc.) might add another $0.05 per minute, thereby permitting the reseller a return on sales of 10 percent on a business requiring almost no investment!

Immediately after WATS resale went into effect, an entire industry of resellers sprang up to take advantage of the new arbitrage opportunities. Companies such as Lexitel, Allnet, and hundreds of others, put together service networks, using not only WATS lines, but also private lines leased from Bell that lowered their costs even further.[7] What made this business so attractive was that not a single transmission facility had to be built; everything could be leased from Bell. Even more ironic, companies such as MCI who owned network facilities connecting certain major cities could now vastly expand their coverage by adding WATS lines to their network. Previously, if a Sprint customer wished to call a town outside Sprint's network, he or she would have been out of luck. Now, Sprint could add a WATS line and complete their customers' calls to anywhere in the country, courtesy of Bell's ubiquitous system. In a single stroke, the specialized carriers' ability to compete increased enormously.

But if Bell had a chance to revise its WATS tariff before resale went into effect, why didn't it modify the rate schedule to eliminate these arbitrage opportunities? AT&T did indeed increase WATS rates for heavy-usage lines, which eliminated some, but not all, arbitrage possibilities. However, large business customers, retail users of WATS, suddenly found their monthly bills doubling. AT&T was limited in how much it could raise WATS rates by how much it could afford to alienate its largest and most valued customers. And there is no doubt that these customers felt misused—for the first time, outraged large users banded together to represent their interests in Washington, only to find that the WATS resale deal was concluded. However, large users now realized that Bell could no longer be depended upon to look after their interests, and they became a new and significant player in the regulatory game with the FCC.

With these two major actions, CI-2 and WATS resale, the FCC had removed some major barriers that prospective long-distance entrants might face, and in a way that made it tough for Bell to cross-subsidize. However, the most difficult problem lay ahead: ensuring competitors' access to Bell's customers.

Access: The Nub of the Problem

Despite the enormous technical advances that had occurred since the invention of the telephone—phone conversations are now bounced off satellites and switched by digital computers—there is one piece of the telecommunications system that is still pretty much as it was in Alexander Bell's day: the pair of copper wires (that is, the electrical connection) from the customer's home, office, or factory to the telephone company's local switching office. In almost all cases, this is a metallic path dedicated to a particular customer, travelling along underground cable or overhead telephone wires. While these access lines usually travel in a common sheath, each customer's line (or "local loop") is separate and distinct from its neighbor. This low-tech component of a high-tech business accounted for approximately one-third of the Bell System's gross investment.[8] The only way for a customer to gain access to the telephone network, including competitors' networks, is through that access line. And, for all the talk about competition, the market for the access line was, circa 1981, a virtually complete monopoly. Running lines under the streets is not what MCI and the interconnect manufacturers are all about. To make their products useful, these competitors need access to the customers' dedicated lines.

As costly as this portion of the telephone system is, the goal of universal service dictated that the price for telephone service be kept low. As a consequence, the price of local service was kept below the historical costs of providing it. Of course, no firm likes to maintain money-losing services, and local telephone companies, both Bell and independent, needed a source of revenues to cover this potential deficit. As discussed in Chapter 1, a complex "separations and settlements" process was put into place to pay local operating companies part of the long-distance revenues as compensation for use of the access line as well as local switching and transmission facilities.

While payments to local operating companies for the use of facilities such as switches and trunk circuits makes obvious economic sense, payments for the fixed access line are economically more suspect. The economic rationale was that Bell offered local service and toll service, and the access line is a joint cost, so its cost should be shared between the two services. The political rationale was that it spread the benefits of innovation in toll switching and transmission to all services in the form of lower prices, kept local rates (about which regulators were most likely to hear complaints) low, and funneled money to small, high-cost independent companies, which were seen as having substantial rural political clout in state legislatures. The philosophical rationale was, of course, universal service.

By 1980, however, the flow of dollars from interstate toll alone was enormous. Even though interstate long-distance only accounted for about 8 percent of the access line usage, approximately 25 percent of the cost of the access line was recovered from long-distance. About one-third of all interstate-toll revenues went back to the operating companies just to help pay for customer access lines. A roughly equal sum was raised from intrastate toll revenues. The burden on toll rates to support local access was equivalent to a "tax" of about 50 percent of sales.

Now if everyone with a telephone access line did the same amount of toll calling, it would not matter so much whether they paid for their access line costs directly or via a "tax" on toll. But there is enormous variation in each customer's amount of toll usage. Compare, for example, a telephone in a ski cabin, used only a few weeks a year and never for toll calls, with the telephone of a family with three children in distant colleges, which may be used five hours a month for long-distance. Both households pay the same monthly rate, but one generates no interstate revenues, while the other generates a huge amount. Each may have its monthly line charges reduced by $10 per month below cost as a result of this revenue flow, but the vacation home customer pays none of the toll "tax," where the tuition-strapped parents must pay nearly $40 per month. For business users, the "tax" can amount to as much as $1500 per month per line, which extra expense is passed on to consumers through higher prices and to stockholders through lower dividends. Clearly, the high-usage customer loses substantially, while the low-usage customer gains.

Another beneficiary of this process is any long-distance carrier who doesn't have to pay the "tax." Immediately after the *Execunet* decision, MCI and others were in this privileged position. Bell quickly filed a tariff for "Exchange Network Facilities for Interstate Access" (ENFIA), by which Execunet-type services would be charged a much higher rate for their local access lines to cover their "fair share," in other words, they would be paying the same effective toll "tax" as Bell for customer-access lines.

The competitive carriers objected to the tariff, which would practically triple (they claimed) the amount they would have to pay Bell for use of its local distribution facilities. Their arguments:

Since the lines the competitive carriers leased from the operating company were physically identical to the lines of any other business customer, they should pay the same tariffed rate.

The tariff was predatory and anticompetitive, the long-distance version of the connecting device that Bell had attempted to force on terminal equipment vendors.

Bell proposed to charge its competitors the full "tax" for access, but, in fact, competitors' access to their customers was far worse than AT&T's. MCI's customers had to dial up to twenty-two digits for each call and were charged for both conversation and ringing time, and MCI had to do its own billing. AT&T customers, on the other hand, dialed at most eleven digits and were only billed for conversation time, and AT&T had the operating companies to do its billing.

If the new rates went into effect, even the most profitable of the new carriers, MCI, would become a money-loser.

Confusion over the very terms of the controversy illustrates the differences that separated the parties. Bell saw access in terms of *facilities*: a piece of hardware, the local loop, that amounted to one-third of Bell's gross plant and had to be paid for, in part, out of toll revenues. If the competitive carriers wanted some of the toll market, they ought to pay their share of these costs. The competitive carriers, however, saw access in terms of *service*: how convenient it was for their customers to get to them, and how easy it was for them to get to their customers.

The competitive carriers were not about to let Bell snatch back the fruits of their Execunet victory by imposing the full toll "tax." The FCC, unwilling to go through interminable evidentiary hearings, suggested that the parties negotiate an agreement, which they could then approve. Negotiations between Bell and the other carriers were carried out under the aegis of the FCC. In December

1978, an agreement was reached according to which the competitive carriers would pay less than 35 to 45 percent of Bell's toll "tax." Bell felt the FCC was granting the other carriers a 20-percent price advantage at Bell's expense; the other carriers still thought Bell was extracting tribute from them for the privilege of access to their customers.

By the early 1980s, the issue of access, separations and settlements, and the competitive exposure of Bell's core of services had moved to center stage. Since 1982, access has dominated the debate on rates, costs, and intercompany funds flow, both before and particularly after the 1984 divestiture. However, in 1979, the very word "access" was strange and new to old telephone hands. The received wisdom was that the local loop is a joint cost, the burden of which was to be shared between local service and toll service, as in *Smith v. Illinois.* Even the brightest minds at AT&T had difficulty, as I witnessed, in grasping the concept of "access" as a service unto itself, with its own identifiable costs, to be charged for separately. They would soon learn.

In fact, the OCC's and some economists (see Noll [1984] for an early exposition of this view) questioned whether or not access was actually priced below its economic (as opposed to historical accounting) cost. They correctly pointed out that what the Bell System had on its books as the "cost" of access was an accounting amalgam of original cost of facilities that may or may not have actually been needed to provide access, that may or may not have been efficiently engineered for this application, and that may or may not have been depreciated to reflect its economic life. The economic cost of access would be the *forward-looking incremental* cost of providing the access function with the latest technology. In principle, the economic cost may be less than the historical accounting cost, perhaps less than the monthly rates the Bell System charged subscribers. Should this be the case, then the flow of dollars from long-distance service to local access was not a subsidy to local-only subscribers: it was a subsidy to Bell stockholders to remunerate them for their management's failure to adequately depreciate these assets! Naturally, the OCC's took this position, claiming that, far from subsidizing the access line, the ENFIA "tax" supported Bell's past errors in underdepreciating its local exchange assets.

How should we assess the claim that the economic cost of access was really below the monthly rate charged by Bell (which in turn, all agreed, was below the historical accounting cost of access)? If the forward-looking incremental cost to provide access were truly below the monthly rates Bell charged, then wouldn't an MCI or a Sprint find it profitable to be a supplier of access lines as well as a long-distance provider? If the economic costs of access were below Bell's monthly rate, then why didn't any OCC choose to enter the market? As a long-distance carrier, they could have provided access at the forward-looking incremental (to their network) cost, which was claimed to be less than the going rate. Since they chose not to do so, we can conclude that the OCC's actually saw the economic cost of providing access greater than the revenues to be realized. While their lawyers argued that long-distance did not provide a subsidy to the access market (which by implication must therefore be profitable on an incremental basis), their business managers, by choosing not to enter the access market, gave lie to this argument.

The Bell Response

By 1981, Bell was staggering from the succession of body blows delivered in the policy arena. The internal view was that regulatory, legal, and legislative activity was no longer aimed at victory — it was damage control, pure and simple. The policy debate was clearly coming to a climax; the only question for Bell was how bad the result would be. In 1979, John deButts turned over the chairman position to Charles Brown, a quiet insider from Illinois Bell, whose earlier work in implementing AT&T's budget-commitment process had helped deButts control independent-minded operating-company presidents so that overall corporate targets could be met. Brown's job was twofold: make peace between the Bell System and Washington, which deButts, with his reputation for stubbornness, could not now negotiate and prepare the firm for the anticipated rigors of the new competitive era.

Internal Transformation

Brown's first thrust was to begin to shift the firm's orientation from an operations/service ethic to a marketing/competitive mindset. The Bell system instituted a major corporate reorganization, away from functional lines (plant, traffic, commercial, etc.) toward market lines (switched network service, CPE, etc.). Marketing executives, primarily from the computer industry, had been brought into the firm some years before, to "change the corporate culture"; now these executives were given the resources and the clout to change Bell's basic corporate strategy. The new marketeers had the highest-level support, and Bell's senior executives went to great pains to communicate the word to the troops: We are going to be market-driven.

The pain caused to an employee body nurtured on the service-to-the-public ethic of the old Bell System was felt from the top to the very bottom of the organization. The tremors of change were felt from the installer in the field to the researcher at Bell Labs. Although they tried to be team players, many employees at all levels felt betrayed, believing the new direction ran counter to their strongly held values.

Brown's instincts were on target: Bell's value structure had to be changed if the firm was to succeed in whatever the new world was to be. Bell's performance in the CPE market indicated it had a long way to go to be an effective, unprotected competitor. Management and employees must value marketplace success for a firm to succeed. Technical expertise and operational efficiency cannot be ends in themselves; they must be translated into competitive advantage, and everyone in a firm must internalize that value for the firm to succeed. Brown administered the first of the many necessary and painful shocks that the employee body would take over the next several years. But this was the first, the loss of innocence, and it hurt.

External Transformation

While these internal problems of organization and motivation were being handled at Bell, Brown's other objective, to make peace with Washington, was far from his grasp. He had assumed that Bell would be thrust into a competitive world with the likes of IBM, Rolm, MCI, and others and would have to learn their ways. Instead, it looked like the Bell of the future would be so tightly constrained from competing that learning competitive ways was fruitless. Each successive congressional bill called for greater limitations on Bell, surer safeguards against anticompetitive and predatory use of its power in monopoly markets to cross-subsidize its competitive ventures. While others feared Bell would play Goliath, Bell feared it would be forced to play Gulliver.

Since the days of Vail, AT&T's commitment to universal service had gradually, imperceptibly, changed from a strategy of accommodation to a fixed policy, then to a belief structure permeating the Bell System. The tragedy of it all is that AT&T employees, in my experience, believed in the Bell System's "Unusual Obligation," as John deButts (1973) termed it, to serve the nation. What regulators, competitors, economists, and policy analysts saw as blatantly anticompetitive behavior, Bell employees and managers alike considered their almost sacred obligation to protect their mission in the public interest. To Bell managers, competitors were cheap dollar-mongerers, concerned with their own interests, rather than the public's. Economists were seen as seeking to impose an economic conception, the competitive marketplace, on an industry where it clearly didn't belong, solely on the grounds of professional dogma. Not only did AT&T's employees not see themselves as anticompetitive and predatory, they regarded themselves as more high-minded and, at the same time, more practical than their tormentors.

By 1981, however, it had become painfully obvious even to Bell's top echelon that this view would not prevail, nor was even a reasonable compromise possible. As his predecessor did seven years before, Brown seemed to be looking for a single stroke of managerial genius that would cut this Gordian knot, so much more complicated than that facing John deButts in 1974. At the end of 1981, he found what he thought was the way out—a negotiated settlement with Justice of the antitrust case.

Notes

1. Robert Bruce, an advocate of regulatory reform, had been appointed FCC general counsel in 1977; Nina Cornell, an economist critical of regulation, headed the FCC's Office of Plans and Policies.
2. The cost manual work continued under a new docket, and the USOA work kept moving, and, of course, Bell's responses to those efforts took on a life of their own. No doubt even as you read these words, cost analysts and accountants at the FCC and AT&T Communications are refining the cost manual, collecting the data, and arguing whether or not it supports their case.

3. Falsely, I believe. The FCC acted with dispatch to solve a nearly unsolvable problem, while the House and Senate dithered.
4. For example, in the highly competitive key systems market, Bell's ComKey product line was essentially 1950s technology, while other firms were bringing electronic programmable systems to market at far better prices than Bell.
5. The material on Execunet is drawn largely from Brock (1981).
6. The approximate cost of a "Full Business Day" WATS line in 1980.
7. Clearly, private line tariffs without resale restrictions held similar problems for Bell. Such restrictions had been removed in 1976; subsequently, Bell withdrew the Telpak tariff, over customer objections.
8. This includes wire and cable, some central office connections, and station connections at the customer's premises (Meyer et al. 1980: Table B-3).

References

AT&T. "Prices and Services—Subscriber Reaction to Copy Statements (Illinois)." In *Hearing before the Subcommittee on Antitrust and Monopoly of the Committee on the Judiciary,* U.S. Senate, 93d Cong., pt. 5, pp. 3455–3459 (1974).

Brock, Gerald. 1981. *The Telecommunications Industry.* Cambridge, Mass.: Harvard University Press.

deButts, John (AT&T chairman). 1973. Speech presented to the National Association of Regulatory Utility Commissioners, September 20. Reprinted in *Heritage and Destiny,* by A. von Auw. New York: Praeger, 1983.

H.R. 13015, 95th Cong., 2d sess. (1978).

Meyer, J.R., R.W. Wilson, M.A. Baughcum, E. Burton, and L. Caouette. 1980. *The Economics of Competition in the Telecommunications Industry.* Cambridge, Mass.: Oelgeschlager, Gunn, and Hain.

Noll, R. 1984. "Comment." In *Telecommunication Access and Public Policy,* edited by M.A. Baughcum and G.R. Faulhaber, p. 142. Norwood, N.J.: Ablex Publishing.

von Auw, A. 1983. *Heritage and Destiny.* New York: Praeger.

CHAPTER 5

The Debate Resolved:
The Divestiture Decision

During the period of 1974 to 1981, the rate of regulatory change increased a hundredfold over the previous decade. The strategy of delay that Bell had practiced so successfully since *Above 890* was no longer possible. Congress was the wild card in the game; unable to pass legislation, its actions still demanded the attention of Bell, the FCC, the other carriers, and a host of lobbyists for potentially affected firms. The Justice Department's antitrust case was in the hands of Judge Greene, who was determined to show the world that the court system could handle a huge antitrust case in a reasonable period of time. Although both sides had shifted their basic positions several times, and Justice's legal personnel were turning over rather quickly, the case was lurching toward the trial opening.

The Machineries of Justice, Continued

Curiously, the Justice Department's antitrust case had gone rather poorly during the late 1970s. Outnumbered by AT&T's lawyers and hampered by staff changes, Justice's cadre of attorneys could not effectively prosecute a case that had only weak support from the Carter administration. In fact, after Carter's defeat in 1980, Justice offered a favorable settlement to AT&T, involving only a "token divestiture" (Derthick and Quirk 1985). At one point, both sides asked Judge Greene to postpone the taking of evidence to give them a chance to reach agreement. Greene, anxious to demonstrate that he could keep the proceedings moving along briskly, was visibly annoyed at this request and limited the postponement to a very short period of time. Perhaps confident that the incoming

Reagan administration would be more sympathetic to its needs, AT&T turned down the offer. The case went to trial on January 15, 1981.

President Reagan's assistant attorney general for antitrust was indeed a conservative—a procompetitive conservative from academia, trained not only in law but also in economics. William Baxter brought to Washington a general distaste for government intervention in the marketplace, in particular for meddlesome antitrust cases, a view he expressed strongly in print (Baxter 1977). In the same article, however, Baxter made it clear that the AT&T case was an exception; he believed that the case should be prosecuted vigorously, with the aim of divestiture of the local loop monopoly to prevent cross-subsidization of competitive services. Only in this way could market forces work to the public's benefit in telecommunications. He explicitly rejected Bell's long-standing subsidy of local-exchange service by long-distance to enhance universal service.

Whatever Mr. Reagan hoped for when he appointed Professor Baxter, what he got was an antitrust chief with specific designs on AT&T, who was forceful enough in cabinet meetings to override the objections of Commerce and Defense to pursuing the case. His widely quoted commitment to "litigate the case to the eyeballs" (*New York Times* 1981) gave new life to the moribund case, and under his leadership the government's prospects brightened considerably. AT&T's decision in late 1980 to wait for a better deal from the incoming Republican regime suggests that they mistakenly believed that "conservative" meant probusiness, or at least pro-Bell, rather than procompetitive. Their lesson in comparative ideology was costly beyond measure.

The presentation of Justice's case, involving almost one hundred witnesses and thousands of documents, took about four months. Following the presentation, AT&T lawyers moved for dismissal on the grounds that Justice had not demonstrated a right to relief. On September 11, 1981, Judge Greene issued an opinion and ruling, denying AT&T's motion to dismiss. The opinion necessarily reviewed Greene's initial views of the government's case and must have shaken AT&T's attorneys considerably. As but one example of the tone of the opinion, Greene found

. . .a persuasive showing has been made that defendants have monopoly power (wholly apart from FCC orders with respect to interconnection)

through various barriers to entry, such as bottlenecks, entrenched customer preferences, the regulatory process, large capital requirements, access to technical information, and disparities in risk.... The testimony ...adduced by the government demonstrated that the Bell System has violated the antitrust laws in a number of ways over a lengthy period of time. (*U.S. v. AT&T* 1981: 12)

AT&T's case was on its way down the tubes. Facing the prospect of treble-damage private suits that would ride the coattails of a Justice victory, Chairman Brown had to act.

The Fateful Decision

In late 1981, AT&T and Sidley & Austin attorneys began another series of negotiations with Justice, this time aimed less at reasonable compromise than at getting out of the case with a whole coat of skin. Brown had decided to cut his losses and settle, on Justice's terms if necessary.

On January 8, 1982, Charles Brown and Assistant Attorney General for Antitrust William Baxter jointly announced settlement of the case, essentially on the terms Justice had sought.[1] AT&T agreed to divest itself of its local operating companies, while retaining long-distance service and all competitive services within AT&T. The local operating companies would continue to be responsible for providing customer access lines, plus some local switching and trunking, which the phone company called "exchange service."

In the excitement of the days following this stunning announcement, Brown outlined at an AT&T management meeting (at which I was present) what he thought he had bought with this settlement:

Bell operating companies would become the local access monopolies, retaining all "exchange" operations within their control and possibly some intrastate short-haul toll traffic;

The operating companies would be required to install facilities to provide equal access to all interexchange (long-distance) carriers; no longer would AT&T be easier to reach than MCI and Sprint;

Long-distance toll, Yellow Pages, CPE, and all new competitive services would be offered by AT&T;

There was some confusion on Brown's part about whether the new cellular mobile-phone service, soon to be introduced, would be offered by the new AT&T or by the divested operating companies (the settlement was specific: it went with the operating companies);

Brown promised employees that the settlement would remove the doubt surrounding the future of the telecommunications industry and that AT&T would be free to compete on an equal footing in all markets, and "capitalize...on future marketplace opportunities" (Brown 1984: 4); and

The restrictions of the 1956 decree were removed, the case would be immediately dismissed, and Justice would supervise the implementation of the settlement.

Brown believed his agreement with Justice had finally solved the fundamental policy dilemma: how to assure that Bell would not abuse its monopoly position in some markets to throttle new entrants in competitive markets. There would no longer be any need for regulators and Congress to be concerned with Bell's incentives to cross-subsidize from monopoly to competitive markets, since there were no monopoly markets left in AT&T. As Brown put it, "[the divestiture] should remove concerns about our using revenues from monopoly services to subsidize competitive offerings" (1984: 5). Brown thought Justice strongly supported this position, since, after all, it had been theirs all along: "...divestiture would also remove remaining restrictions on the ability of interexchange carriers to compete effectively in the provision of ordinary long-distance services...[and] eliminate the...source of potential cross-subsidization as well" (United States Department of Justice 1982: 35).

With the full support of its former antagonist, Brown expected that Bell would soon be able to compete in any market, unfettered by the handicaps and constraints previously felt necessary to limit its market power. Justice's view on the need for continued regulation:

Moreover, because of the removal of AT&T's incentives and abilities to monopolize exchange services, the prospects for the deregulation of that market will be enhanced. With the dissipation of AT&T's market power in an increasing number of interexchange markets, the need for regulatory intervention will erode sharply in the coming years (United States Department of Justice 1982: 35).

Greene Takes Control

Brown believed, as did Baxter at Justice, that the matter had been taken out of Judge Greene's court. Both sides knew that the Antitrust Procedures and Penalties Act (Tunney Act) required that all consent decrees between Justice and any plaintiff be subject to a court-conducted inquiry to determine if the decree was "in the public interest," a highly uncertain process that could take months. Justice and AT&T apparently tried to avoid this delay by casting the settlement not as a consent decree, but as a modification of the "Final Judgment" consent decree of the 1956 antitrust case. Since the "Modification of Final Judgment" (MFJ) was merely an alteration of an existing agreement, it was hoped—although both sides later denied this—that it would not be subject to the Tunney Act procedures.

AT&T and Justice requested that responsibility for the 1956 consent decree be moved from Newark, New Jersey, to Greene's court in Washington, D.C.. After some embarrassment when the New Jersey judge wanted to sign the decree right away, the transfer was made (*U.S. v. AT&T* 1982). Both parties let Greene know that they believed he could sign the MFJ and walk away from the case; they underestimated Greene's interest. Greene announced that he didn't know whether or not the Tunney Act applied, but he would certainly go through its procedures. In other words, Greene used the authority of the bench to keep control of the case, as well as control of the final economic outcome (Shooshan 1984: 18).

Harold Greene, an experienced jurist, inherited the case when his predecessor, Judge Waddy, died in 1976. At the time, the system was being roundly criticized for its inept handling of the huge IBM case, in litigation since 1969 with almost zero progress. Publicly committed to firm case management, Greene let the parties know he would brook no delay. As the case wore on, Greene gained a reputation, at least among the Bell and Sidley & Austin lawyers, for not being shy about expressing opinions on the merits of the contending arguments. Greene gave the impression of strong interest in the case and of confidence in his own competence to come to judgment on the issues. This was not a man intimidated by large institutions or executive power. This was not a man who was about to relinquish the power to reshape the Bell System according to his definition of the public interest.

Divestiture Is *Not* Deregulation

The settlement momentarily stunned the Washington policy community, but it quickly recovered. The Senate Subcommittee on

Communications, Science, and Transportation held hearings on the settlement, and Brown called in his chit with Baxter, who testified that he believed the new AT&T's markets to be "workably competitive" (Baxter 1982). In the weeks following the announcement, Baxter repeatedly expressed his hopes for early deregulation of the new AT&T. Yet Brown's expectations and Baxter's rhetoric had no discernible effect on anyone who might actually have done something about deregulation. The FCC said that it was still studying the matter and intended to go ahead with business as usual, implementing CI-2, etc.

After the early euphoria, it slowly dawned on the participants that the settlement did not eliminate or even modify a single regulation that applied to AT&T or the operating companies. State and federal regulators possessed precisely the same statutory power over the industry as before, and they intended to use it. Nor was the settlement taken by legislators to mean that there was no need for legislation or further restrictions on AT&T. In the House, Tim Wirth was gearing up for hearings to determine what legislation was appropriate in the light of the AT&T–Justice settlement.

Throughout the 1970s, the policy debate had focused on the question of cross-subsidization. This ostensible concern had led the FCC and Congress to consider special restrictions and handicaps that would limit Bell's ability and incentives for predation. Brown thought that the issue had been laid to rest by the settlement. He was essentially correct, but he had failed to recognize that others would continue to view AT&T's market power in long-distance and switching and transmission systems as a potential threat. Contrary to his belief, removing the need for restrictions, regulations, and handicaps would not automatically result in the removal of those restrictions, regulations, and handicaps that were hampering AT&T's ability to compete.

Brown's expectations were quite reasonable in view of the regulatory and legislative rhetoric. However, they were quite *un*reasonable in view of the regulatory and legislative reality. AT&T's competitors, now such effective participants in the regulatory game, had an obvious interest in hobbling Bell. From the standpoint of an MCI, a GTE, or an equipment manufacturer, the more limits on Bell, the more profits for them. Any imagined possible abuse by Bell that could be translated into a restrictive law or regulation was in their interest to advance. Just as, a decade earlier, Bell claimed "harms to the network" to keep out competitors, so now its competitors claimed "the need to protect competition" to justify handicapping Bell in their markets. Policymakers' legitimate concerns about Bell's market power were simply grist for the mill of competitors seeking market advantage through the regulatory game. Eliminating those concerns did not eliminate the incentives of AT&T's competitors, nor did it convince regulators to eliminate their own jobs. After the settlement, the regulatory demand for handicapping was still high; new rationales simply replaced those that had been made obsolete. The testimony of Brophy, the chairman of GTE, in which he suggested to Congress ways to handicap AT&T and the BOC's to "protect competition," offers an almost classic example of special pleading to seek economic advantage at a competitor's expense through the regulatory and legislative processes (1982: 326–343). This is not a criticism of Mr. Brophy or the dozens of other interested parties who sought restrictions on AT&T in their markets. Their responsibility is to their shareholders; if the political and regulatory process permits them to increase their earnings through restrictions on their competitors, they would be derelict in their duties should they not take advantage of such an opportunity. Similarly, when Bell saw opportunities in the 1960s and early 1970s to further its corporate goals through regulatory delays, it did not hesitate to exploit them. The problem, from the point of view of the nation's economic well-being, is not the players, it's the game. The regulatory/legislative game was absorbing enormous resources, both public and private, in order to inhibit competitors—and therefore competition—in an industry that needed all the competition it could get.

Charles Brown apparently believed that the settlement with Justice ended the regulatory game and that the telephone company could get on with its business. In fact, the game continued. The settlement was just another move, albeit a massive one, in the continuous jockeying for political advantage that characterizes markets subject to public control.

The Theory of the Case: How It Might Have Worked

The terms of the settlement—divestiture of the exchange business from CPE, long-distance, and other more competitive parts of the firm—were not a random punishment that Justice had decided to inflict upon Bell. The settlement followed from Justice's underlying theory of what was wrong with this market, laid out in Baxter (1977), and more recently discussed in Brennan (1986). In brief, this was a vertical foreclosure case: Bell had used its monopoly control over customer access lines to restrict, inhibit, and otherwise interfere with the other long-distance carriers' need to gain access to customers through those lines. Bell's control over this bottleneck facility enabled it to extend its market power into the long-distance market, by ensuring better access to Bell long-distance than to MCI, Sprint, or any of the other carriers. Moreover, it had used its monopoly over customer access lines to restrict providers of CPE from selling equipment that their customers could connect to those lines.

Justice's solution was simple: *Separate the monopoly access market of Bell (exchange service) from the competitive (CPE) and potentially competitive (long-distance) markets of Bell.* This would completely remove any incentive to use the local access line as a weapon in the battle for long-distance, either by restricting access or by cross-subsidizing.

The exchange companies, regulated by the states, would offer only monopoly access and exchange service. It would be in their interest to offer equal access to all long-distance carriers, rather than to favor one (AT&T) over any other. It would also be in their interest to ensure that all CPE would work effectively, not just Western Electric's. Since the exchange companies would not be involved in any other business, they could concentrate on providing the best exchange service. They would fare best if their customers used as much service as possible, which could be encouraged by providing as many long-distance and CPE options as possible.

AT&T, no longer under suspicion of denying its competitors access to the bottleneck access lines, would be able to enter any market it wished and would be free (eventually) to price its products and services with equal freedom. AT&T and its vaunted technology would be unleashed to help drive the coming information age, unfettered (eventually) by regulatory handicaps.

The competitive long-distance carriers, no longer disadvantaged by inferior access, would be free to take on AT&T in the long-distance market. Consumers, rather than regulators, could soon choose the right long-distance carrier for them.

Providers of switching and transmission gear would now be able to compete for the huge BOC market on an equal basis with a Western Electric no longer affiliated with the operating companies.

Certainly Justice's solution promised a bright future for competitors, AT&T, and consumers. But how did it stack up against the political realities of regulatory subsidies? The divestiture would disrupt the financial arrangements of separations and settlements. Since AT&T and the Bell Operating Companies were now separate firms, the old procedures were no longer adequate. However, it was a straightforward matter to continue the subsidy, should regulators wish to do so, even though the two parts of the business were now in separate firms. Instead of the old separations and settlements mechanism for the transfer of funds, the BOC's could establish a tariff for carrier access in excess of the actual cost of providing connections by an amount equal to the old subsidy. The long-distance carriers would then see the tariff as payment to the BOC's for the right to hook up to their switches. All costs assigned by the BOC's to interstate service via separations, including the subsidy to the access line, could thus be recovered. The only difference would be that, predivestiture, the funds transfer was internal to the Bell System; postdivestiture, the funds transfer occurred under tariff.[2]

The possibility of using carrier access charges to continue the subsidy flow from long-distance to local, from AT&T to the BOC's, was recognized at the time of the settlement by both AT&T and Justice, as well as by the FCC. Many others, including some state regulators and opportunistic legislators, either did not understand this basic fact of the business or, knowing it, chose anyway to capitalize on the public's confusion by announcing that the divestiture would necessarily increase subscribers' monthly rates two to three times. It is ironic that one of the most well-planned aspects of the MFJ should have been the most misunderstood.

The Theory of the Case: How It Might Have Failed

There were three major flaws in Justice's master plan, two related to its economics and one to its politics:

1. The structural distinction between monopoly and competitive markets was at best an approximation, critically depen-

dent on the technologies deployed to provide service. Those technologies change rapidly—an industry split into monopoly and competitive components based on today's supply characteristics will in all likelihood be quite inappropriate for the next decade. Already the alleged "natural monopoly" of the operating companies was proving to be temporary. New technologies were emerging that could render obsolete the regulated access monopoly, particularly for highly concentrated users, in a few years.

2. As originally conceived, the exchange companies looked like terrible places for ambitious managers and technocrats. Their future looked to be highly restricted, with only the gradual erosion of their most profitable markets to new technology to look forward to. How viable such companies would have been is unclear.

3. Brown's negotiated settlement was with Justice only and did not include any of the parties that could make deregulation happen, such as Congress, the FCC, or perhaps the White House. Deregulation, or at least absence of restraints and handicaps, was what Brown thought he gave up his company for; but he did not give it up to the people who could actually deliver deregulation, who, in any case, still suspected that AT&T possessed dangerous residual market power in long-distance.

Collectively, these three flaws guaranteed that the MFJ, if implemented, would not lead to the establishment of a competitive marketplace in telecommunications, and the MFJ could not be implemented for political reasons anyway.

Who's Competitive, Who's Monopoly?

Baxter's optimism about the competitiveness of the long-distance market made economic sense, but none politically. The conditions of the MFJ removed AT&T's ability to use its market power in access to control the long-distance market, as well as ensuring that the BOC's would implement the equal access provisions of the decree by 1986. By that time, every telephone customer would have been given an explicit opportunity to choose a principal long-distance carrier. The BOC's would make available the same kinds of access arrangements to all carriers,[3] who would then compete on the basis of their respective merits. As ammunition in the competitive battle, each carrier would be able to engage in advertising and other informational activities prior to each customer's "election day." While waiting for the BOC's to provide equal access, the carriers would be building their reputations for quality, customer service, billing accuracy, and all the other attributes important to customers.

Only if firms were deterred from entry by the need to spend a great deal on sunk costs would this market not be competitive. Yet the capital expenditures on fiber-optic transmission capacity by the new long-distance carriers in the early to mid-1980s suggests that this has not in practice been a barrier to entry. To an economist, then, such a market looks quite competitive. Should a single firm attract a large share, one could only presume that consumers preferred its offerings over its competitors'. Even if AT&T long-distance maintained a large share, the "contestability" (Baumol, Panzar, and Willig 1982) of this market rewards responsiveness to customer needs and tends to squeeze out any monopoly profits for the winners. Politically, however, the existence of a dominant firm with a large market share smacks of *de facto* monopoly, which can be used by less successful competitors to argue for maintaining or increasing restrictions and regulations on the dominant carrier. The mandate of the decree for equal access and the willingness of a number of firms to invest in long-distance facilities strongly suggest that this market is "workably competitive," in the economists' sense of the term. However, the popular perception of a competitive market, generally tied to market share measures, was not fulfilled—the door for continued regulation and demands for handicapping remained open. Justice's view of the access line was stark—access was perceived as the last natural monopoly of the telecommunications system. The *prima facie* evidence seemed to be strong: (1) despite numerous entrants clamoring to get into telephone markets, not a single firm wanted to get into the general local exchange market as an alternate supplier to the BOC's; and (2) having two or more companies provide access lines, local switching centers, and other facilities for local exchange service is "obviously duplicative." Baxter (1982) characterized local exchange as the "inevitably regulated monopoly exchange."

On closer examination, this evidence is far from compelling. First, the long-standing subsidy from long-distance toll to local exchange meant that access was priced significantly below its cost; no sane competitor would enter such a market, and none did. Lack of competitive entry, then, was only evidence that access was heavily subsidized, not that access is a natural monopoly. Second, the technology of access that makes competition "obviously duplicative" is essentially identical to the technology of access at the turn of the century: pairs of twisted copper wire running through cables to the company's central switch. Back then, the expiration of the Bell patents gave rise to strongly rivalrous behavior among independent telephone companies, including substantial price-cutting. If today's regulatory protection were removed, why would we not see similar patterns of competition emerge? History gives the lie to the natural monopoly argument for local access.[4] Further, the very fact that the access technology has remained generally unchanged for the past one hundred years should indicate that regulatory protection, coupled with artificially low rates, is a sure route to technological stagnation. If regulation were abated and prices adjusted to reflect more nearly the costs in this market, we could expect to see innovative access systems developed that could compete with and beat this archaic nineteenth-century access technology. Even before divestiture, there was mounting evidence that the technological base for access competition was in place, just waiting for the opportunity to be exploited (Brock 1984; Baughcum and Faulhaber 1984: Parts II and III). While no one expected competitive entry overnight, it was obvious that the access monopoly would be of limited duration.

Woe Unto the BOC's

From the economists' viewpoint, it would appear that the BOC's were extremely well positioned postdivestiture. They retained the key bottleneck facility—the access line—as their very own monopoly, at least for the short run. This monopoly could be exploited from either side, depending on political expediency: the customer needed the access line to get to suppliers of long-distance, and the suppliers of long-distance needed the access line to get to their customers. Further, the BOC's had a history of playing the regulatory game with their state PUC's, which tended to be strongly anticompetitive. From the technological and economic perspectives, the only cloud on an otherwise sunny horizon was the potential for access competition, or "bypass."

State regulators, BOC employees, and the public, however, saw the divestiture as a disaster. State regulators, aware that the massive flow of separations and settlements dollars kept local rates low, jumped to the conclusion that divestiture would stop that flow, thus causing rates to increase. Within days after the AT&T–Justice settlement was announced, state regulators began telling their constituents that the divestiture meant that the poor BOC's would have to double or triple their rates, since AT&T had abandoned them, and that it was the fault of the courts, not of the state regulators. Of course, this was false, as we'll see below, but misrepresentation is apparently not too high a price to pay for political advantage in the regulatory game.

BOC employees, on the other hand, were genuinely shocked and dismayed. It was normal within the Bell System for BOC employees to chafe under the advice of AT&T and to wish that their "owner" were not so directive. However, employees first reacted to the divestiture announcement as if they were the aggrieved party in a particularly bitter divorce. They felt that AT&T had deserted with all the new, exciting, high-tech services and products, leaving the BOC's only copper wires, telephone poles, and outdated, underdepreciated switching and transmission gear. I recall a particularly painful telephone conversation with an operating company counterpart that took place within weeks of the divestiture announcement. After transacting our business, the BOC man said that he would follow through at his end, "even though we've been abandoned to a dead-end business with all the growth potential of the local water company," and that he hoped I would never have to experience such a shock of rejection.

An amalgam of these reactions emerged through the media. *Time* magazine, after referring to AT&T as "Ma Bell" and to AT&T's separated subsidiary as "Baby Bell," called the BOC's "Grandma Bell," reflecting the perception that the BOC's had been stuck with the old technology and that the MFJ prohibited them from taking a place in the exploding information marketplace heralded by the business press. A widely publicized assertion was that AT&T kept one-third of the assets (and thus one-third of the cost) and two-thirds of the revenues, leaving the BOC's with the short end of the stick. While AT&T went off into deregulated markets to make gobs of money (so the story went), the local operating companies, saddled with antiquated technology, would be struggling to make ends meet, most likely through substantial rate increases.

Of course, in a competitive market, the moral leverage of a firm counts for naught; success comes from meeting the needs of your customers better than anyone else can, not from making people feel sorry for you. However, in the regulatory game, public perceptions of your firm as an underdog can be translated into competitive advantage in the marketplace. The BOC's were to show that they could play this game better than AT&T, at least in Judge Greene's court in 1982.

The Regulatory Game Redux

Perhaps the most serious flaw in Justice's plan to establish a competitive telecommunications market was that it did not include any provision for actually getting rid of regulation. Though the plan removed much of the rationale for continued tight regulation of AT&T, regulators relaxed not a single regulation, and AT&T's competitors continued to claim that they required regulatory protection from AT&T's market power in order to "make competition work."

In at least one way, the divestiture made the regulatory game even more of a quagmire than it already was, by taking one single and very large player, the Bell System, and creating eight new players, AT&T and the BOC holding companies, each quite large in its own right. Within six months, the FCC found itself adjudicating squabbles, not only between the competitive carriers and AT&T, but between AT&T and its soon-to-be-independent subsidiaries, potentially far more damaging to the health of the telephone system.

Of course, it can be argued that deregulation is not Justice's job; their goal should be to break up monopoly power wherever they find it. However, the role that regulators play in establishing and enforcing monopoly suggests that any attempt to deal with monopoly power purely through the firm and not through the regulator is to treat only half the ailment. A standing joke among economists close to the government's case was that (in the Watergate jargon then current) "the FCC is an unindicted co-conspirator."

Perhaps the truth behind the joke should have led Justice to go beyond mere divestiture, to see that the regulatory process invites monopolization (or cartelization), and to strike at the heart of the problem.

Even if deregulation was not Justice's job, it certainly should have been high on Chairman Brown's list. It was certainly his goal to turn AT&T's efforts and attention away from the Washington scene and toward the exciting business opportunities he saw for the firm. As long as the regulatory process was in place, giving ear to special interests with more political than marketplace clout, AT&T would be enmeshed in restrictions and handicaps. What's surprising is that a man acknowledged to be a canny politician could agree to a radical divestiture with no assurance, much less guarantee, that he would get something out of it. In acceding to Justice's terms, Brown could have demanded some sort of *quid pro quo* that would have at least lessened, if not totally eliminated, his regulatory entanglements.

Clearly, any attempt to link deregulatory initiatives with the AT&T–Justice settlement would have required coordination between the executive branch and Congress that was beyond the immediate power of Assistant Attorney General Baxter. However, Baxter had shown himself a savvy and effective politician during early Reagan administration cabinet meetings, when he obtained the backing of the administration for vigorous prosecution of the AT&T case. By late 1981, had Brown demanded it, Baxter might have been able to enlist the support of an immensely popular president, who was having phenomenal luck with Congress at the time. Had the president, Baxter, the FCC, and several key House and Senate members lined up behind procompetitive deregulatory legislation that phased out state and federal regulation, with sufficient safeguards to protect consumers, the nation might well have been on its way to a truly competitive telecommunications marketplace.[5]

It will never be known whether or not the Reagan administration or congressional leadership would have been willing or able to take on the job of coordinating the government's restructuring of the telecommunications industry. Certainly they had plenty on their minds at the time, what with massive tax reductions and the Lebanon crisis. However, the combination of the importance of the Bell System and the most massive antitrust case ever prosecuted by the Justice Department certainly could have exerted a legitimate claim to the attention of the White House and Congress, particularly since the matter affected virtually every individual in the nation. Whether an AT&T–Justice appeal for top-level leadership would have been successful is problematic; the wonder is that such an appeal was never made. The wonder is that Brown apparently didn't even ask that his firm's fate be taken out of the hands of the government's third-stringers—an assistant attorney general, a regulatory commission, and a young House subcommittee chairman.[6] And the wonder is that Brown did not insist that a popular and powerful antiregulatory president and administration provide leadership for a government otherwise unable to coordinate itself, in return for agreeing to divestiture, a price in accord with Justice's theory of the case. Absent executive leadership by those such as Baxter and Brown, the regulatory game will continue; political skills will be more rewarded than will creative products and services.

But while the divestiture decision did not end the regulatory game, it did change the ground rules substantially. It was the ultimate structuralist solution, in that it went beyond separate subsidiaries to complete ownership separation, and it marks the high water of structure-type remedies. It was also the death knell for regulated monopoly. Perhaps most significantly, old Ma Bell began acting as if her life depended upon the ability to compete successfully and, for the first time in a decade, she was right.

In sum, the failure of Justice's theory of the case to deal with the regulatory process ensured that, even if implemented, a competitive telecommunications market was still as far away as ever. The failure to anticipate the strong reaction of sympathy toward the BOC's guaranteed that the plan would not be implemented as it stood. Amid the uproar and confusion occasioned by the settlement announcement, Judge Greene used the power of the bench to seize and keep the whip hand.

Denouement: Judge Greene Cuts a Deal

As more of the details of the AT&T–Justice agreement unfolded, interested parties, such as the state regulators and the newly independent operating companies, began firming up their positions in preparation for Judge Greene's Tunney Act procedures. These hearings were held in Greene's court in the spring and summer of

1982. In keeping with his pretrial promise to keep the case moving, Greene expedited the hearings as well. AT&T and Justice were required to submit tentative plans showing how the divestiture would take place, when it would happen, what assets and services would go to the operating companies, how extensive the "exchange areas" would be, and how the financial liabilities would be distributed, all of this prior to the hearings so that interested parties could comment upon them, and Greene could then "suggest" changes to the settlement agreement.

The interested parties had an opportunity to warm up for Greene's hearings by participating in one last congressional effort to pass legislation. Representative Tim Wirth saw the MFJ as leading to new opportunities for the creation of coalitions. Wirth sought to write a bill that would attract the support of the labor unions — who were concerned about seniority and job rights under reorganization — as well as the soon-to-be-independent Bell operating companies, the newly fearful state commissioners, and AT&T's long-distance and CPE competitors. The bill, HR 5158, would have substantially restricted the new AT&T's ability to compete, in the interest of protecting competitors against cross-subsidy and predation. It would have also ensured continued revenue flows from long-distance services, primarily AT&T's, to the local operating companies. It would have actually prohibited competition in local exchange service (bypass) until 1990. AT&T saw this as a disaster: Not only had it not been deregulated, it looked like it might be more tightly constrained and more heavily taxed than ever before. It launched a massive letter-writing campaign from employees and stockholders to Congress, the theme of which was "let's give the settlement a chance; kill this bill." As one industry observer put it some months later, Bell exercised its considerable ability to mobilize political power that would ensure through divestiture that it would never have such power again. And as opposed to almost all other AT&T political actions of the previous decade, this one worked. HR 5158 disappeared from the telecommunications scene.

But Judge Greene was quite visible that summer, using his bench as a bargaining table with himself as the adjudicator. The soon-to-be-independent operating companies made it clear to Greene that the revenues from their offered services did not come close to covering their costs. The state public utility commissions asked that their operating companies be permitted to retain profitable services such as Yellow Pages in order to defray those costs without raising local rates. Any form of competition that would threaten the maintenance of long-standing subsidies was opposed by consumer groups and state regulators alike. The newspaper industry pleaded (as they had to Congress) that they could not compete with big, bad AT&T in the emerging field of electronic publishing (videotext) and sought to ban AT&T from this market "to protect competition."

Abandoning completely the original conception of the settlement as isolating monopoly markets only with the operating companies, Greene apparently felt his role was to divide up the goodies according to his view of what was equitable. Politically influential newspapers got what they wanted; the operating companies, viewed with sympathy by the public, walked away winners; AT&T, which commanded no public sympathy, gave up much more than it had bargained for, including the Bell name!

In principle, of course, the court has no right to dictate the terms of a consent decree, which is an agreement between the two parties to a litigation. Judge Greene's aggressive use of the Tunney Act, however, put him in the position of determining whether or not the MFJ was "in the public interest." He was thus able to threaten the parties implicitly with nonapproval if they did not agree to his "suggestions." Since the alternative to acquiescence was to reopen litigation before a judge who would likely view nonacquiescence as defiance of his sense of equity, both AT&T and Justice were effectively forced to accept his terms.

As imperfect as was Justice's separation of monopoly and competitive markets, Greene proceeded to muddy things further by remixing clearly competitive businesses back into the monopoly BOC's. Whereas Justice tried to tease apart the monopoly yolk from the competitive whites, Greene busily set about making omelets. How was this done?

> The original settlement sought to isolate the monopoly "exchange service" in the BOC's, "exchange service" being interpreted in the traditional telephone sense to mean the customer's access line, the local switching office, and transmission in the local area and to the toll switch ("class 4 office"), where the BOC would connect with the interexchange carriers. In the revised MFJ, the BOC's were permitted to provide long-distance service within their Local Access and

Transport Areas (LATA), which are far larger than the traditional exchange areas. Each LATA is generally the size of
a large city and its suburbs or even an entire state, such as
Wyoming. Thus, the BOC's retained a substantial amount
of long-distance traffic, which the Justice Department had
argued was "workably competitive."

Yellow Pages, the Bell System's highly profitable directory advertising service, was taken from AT&T and placed with the
BOC's. No one had ever seriously claimed that directory
advertising was a monopoly service, and yet Judge Greene
stated (*U.S. v. AT&T* 1982: Note 2) that Yellow Pages might
well qualify. Besides, Yellow Pages profits could be used as
an offset to keep local rates low.

Similarly, the BOC's were permitted to provide, but not manufacture, CPE, which Greene believed would add to the vigor
of competition in this market. The Bell System's previous
history of using the access monopoly to impede CPE competition was brushed aside by Greene. So also was the fact that
competition in the CPE market was already quite vigorous.

The BOC's were given the exclusive use of the Bell name and
logo; of the subsidiaries of the new AT&T, only Bell Labs
could retain the use of the Bell name.

AT&T was forbidden to enter the electronic-publishing market
for seven years. Greene waxed eloquent in his defense of
small, new competitors who might be "crushed" by AT&T.
In fact, those who are active in establishing the videotext
market are firms such as CBS, the Knight-Ridder newspaper
chain, IBM, and Sears Roebuck.

The BOC's could petition the court to waive the line-of-business
restrictions if they could show that competition in those markets would not be harmed and that such businesses would
constitute no more than 10 percent of the BOC's net revenues.

In an unparalleled burst of hubris, Judge Greene announced
that he would indefinitely maintain jurisdiction over en-
forcement of the decree.

About the only things the operating companies were constrained from were inter-LATA long-distance service, electronic
publishing, and the manufacture of CPE. As of February, 1986,
the BOC's had requested eighty-six waivers and been granted fifty-

three, including real estate, office equipment, lease financing, computers and software, and foreign business ventures (Brennan 1986: 43).

Greene's willingness to permit the operating companies' entry into so many competitive businesses apparently stemmed from his desire to guarantee the BOC's adequate revenues to support local exchange service without substantial increases in local rates. What he seemed to forget was that the BOC's were the inheritors of the monopoly power of the Bell System and had plenty of opportunities to exploit that power:

> The BOC's controlled the long-distance carriers' access to their customers; with carrier access charges, they could continue the toll-to-local subsidy that had so handsomely supported them in the past.
>
> The BOC's had in place a billing and collection system that included every customer who would ever use a long-distance carrier. Unless and until those carriers completed their own billing systems, the BOC's could offer to bill customers for the long-distance carriers at a substantial profit.
>
> The BOC's were the firms that assigned telephone numbers to businesses and listed them in the white pages. Even if Yellow Pages had remained with AT&T, some of the Yellow Pages profit could be captured by the BOC's through the sale to the highest bidder of their updated list of business names, numbers, and addresses.

In short, the BOC's had enough market power to keep them financially solvent without rate increases for exchange service and without the benefit of competitive services and line-of-business waivers. Greene's largesse hardly seemed necessary.

On the other hand, why should we care who got Yellow Pages? Either way, either of two large corporations would offer the service, and it appears of little consequence to consumers which one won. Indeed, why do we care if the BOC's sell office equipment and computer repair services or not?

We care because when Greene allowed BOC's to enter competitive markets even though they controlled the monopoly bottleneck access facility, he recreated the conditions in the old Bell System that led to the 1974 antitrust case in the first place. All the public policy problems that the divestiture was supposed to solve were not solved at all; they were simply moved from the Bell System to the new BOC's. The divestiture decision changed a great deal in the telecommunications industry; what it did not change was the fundamental policy problem when one firm exists in both monopoly and competitive markets. Divestiture, Judge Greene–style, simply relocated the problem. Whatever evils regulators and competitors had found in the Bell System's structure, most remained in the structures of the BOC's.[7]

Of all the parties involved in the AT&T–Justice case, Judge Greene was really riding the crest of the wave. Using the Tunney Act, he had leveraged the power of the bench to preside over the dispute of two litigants into lifetime control over a multibillion dollar industry. He became the *de facto* czar of telecommunications, praised by his colleagues as "...clearly one of the most distinguished federal jurists in our society" (Verveer 1984: 88) and the darling of the business press. Curiously, his actions were seen, not as judicial excess, but as statesmanlike.

Undoubtedly, Judge Greene was motivated by a strong sense of justice, as well as a sense of obligation to see the job through to the best of his abilities, on the basis of the trial record in front of him. Seeing so much evidence of the inability of regulation or legislation to bring order and reason to this industry, Judge Greene could be excused for believing that perhaps he would be able to clarify where others had only obscured. Yet, as others before him with similar intentions and ability, he became part of the problem even as he struggled to be its solution.

Without commenting on the legitimacy of Greene's assumption of power over the industry, we can pass judgment on the results of his use of that power. By the end of summer 1982, Judge Greene had transformed a radical but carefully considered experiment in industrial economics into a radical crapshoot with one of America's essential infrastructure industries as the ante.

Notes

1. At the same time, Justice also announced that it was dropping its longstanding case against IBM. The timing highlighted the strong contrast between the two decisions: in the AT&T case, Justice won virtually everything it asked for; in the IBM case, Justice won nothing, abandoning its case.
2. A substantial external funds transfer also occurred from AT&T to the independent telephone companies. After divestiture, the independents, too, adopted carrier access charges, and the entire settlements process was abandoned.

3. There could be a menu of options, each option available to all long-distance carriers.
4. The fact that less than 10 percent of households subscribed to exchange service in this period might suggest that there was more room for competition back then. What is far more likely is that in the 1890s Bell and its independent rivals were competing for the *same* 5–10 percent of the population that could afford to subscribe.
5. Many observers would disagree that at this late date Brown had any bargaining power at all with Justice. Some have argued that Bell's last chance to cut a deal was with Congress in 1979; others aver that Bell blew it in 1976, when Congress felt tricked by CCRA (the Bell bill).
6. As an example of a card not played, recall that Baxter and the Antitrust Division had already made the internal decision to drop the IBM case. The chairman of the House Subcommittee on Telecommunications, Tim Wirth, represented a Colorado district with a strong IBM presence. Surely a Baxter offer to drop a major antitrust case against one of Wirth's major constituents could have led to his help in passing a procompetitive and antihandicapping communications legislation that would have given AT&T a *quid pro quo* for agreeing to divestiture.
7. Brennan (1986) gives a lucid and compelling account of how Greene's modifications of the MFJ turned a structural solution into a structural nonsolution.

References

Baughcum, M.A., and G.R. Faulhaber, eds. 1984. *Telecommunications Access and Public Policy*. Norwood, N.J.: Ablex Publishing.

Baumol, W.J., J.C. Panzar, and R.D. Willig. 1982. *Contestable Markets and the Theory of Industry Structure*. New York: Harcourt Brace Jovanovich.

Baxter, W.F. 1977. "How Government Cases Get Selected—Comments from Academia." *American Bar Association Antitrust Law Journal*, Spring: 586–601.

———. 1982. "Statement." Given before the Senate Subcommittee on Communications, Science, and Transportation, February 4.

Brennan, T. 1986. "Regulated Firms in Unregulated Markets: Understanding the Divestiture in *U.S. v. AT&T*." EAG Discussion Paper 86-5, Antitrust Division, U.S. Department of Justice, Washington, D.C.

Brock, G.W. 1984. "Bypass of the Local Exchange: A Quantitative Assessment." OPP Working Paper 12, Federal Communications Commission, Washington, D.C.

Brophy, T.F. 1982. "Statement before the House Subcommittee on Telecommunications, Consumer Protection and Finance." In *The AT&T Settlement: Terms, Effects, Prospects*. New York: Law & Business, Inc.

Brown, C.L. 1984. "A Personal Introduction." In *Disconnecting Bell*, edited by Harry M. Shooshan, III. Elmsford, N.Y.: Pergamon Press.

Derthick, M., and P.J. Quirk. 1985. *The Politics of Deregulation*. Washington: The Brookings Institution.

New York Times. 1981. April 10, pp. A1, D3.

Shooshan, Harry M., III. 1984. "The Bell Breakup: Putting It In Perspective." In *Disconnecting Bell*, edited by Harry M. Shooshan, III. Elmsford, N.Y.: Pergamon Press.

United States Department of Justice. *Competitive Impact Statement in Connection With Proposed Modification of Final Judgment*, 47 F.R. 7170, 7176 (1982).

United States v. AT&T, 524 F. Supp. 1336, 1381 (D.D.C. 1981)("Opinion on AT&T's Motion to Dismiss").

———. 552 F. Supp. 131 (1982)("Modification of Final Judgment").

Verveer, P. 1984. "Regulation and the Access Problem: What's Happened and Where We are Now." In *Telecommunications Access and Public Policy*, edited by M.A. Baughcum and G.R. Faulhaber, pp. 83–88. Norwood, N.J.: Ablex Publishing.

CHAPTER 6

The Economics of
Telecommunications

At this critical juncture in the story of the telecommunications industry, we turn to a discussion of the economic principles that govern both regulation and antitrust and examine how they were applied in the tumultuous public policy debates leading up to and including the divestiture. The putative policy problem that occupied center stage during this debate was how regulation could limit the potential for anticompetitive practices by a firm operating in both monopoly and competitive markets. We must understand the economics of regulated monopoly and antitrust as applied to telecommunications in order to judge how effectively the problem was resolved.

The Economics of Regulated Monopoly

Prior to 1959, this industry that many today see as potentially competitive was universally considered as appropriately a regulated monopoly. Why would we expect a nation founded on the principle of Natural Liberty, whose antitrust laws are a unique commitment to free competition, ever to regulate private economic behavior? Broadly speaking, our institutionalized faith in the free market derives from the fundamental theorem that, under certain general conditions, the voluntary exchange of goods and services by persons acting in their own self-interest will lead society to a maximum use of its limited resources. According to this concept, the competitive market is efficient because, through it, society's resources are used to the fullest to satisfy the needs and desires of its members. Since exchange is voluntary, all parties to each transaction are better off than they would have been had the transaction not occurred (but not, perhaps, by as much as they might wish). In a competitive market, *all* mutually beneficial trades occur, and *only* mutually beneficial trades occur.

But an important corollary to this theorem is that the conditions under which this excellent state of affairs obtains are by no means universal. In many bargaining situations and in certain industries, conditions are not conducive to an efficient allocation of scarce resources; economists refer to these as "market failures." Government intervention in the form of regulation is one means by which such market failures can be corrected. Antitrust activities are another. From the purely economic perspective, government intervention can be justified if there is a market failure, and the intervention has a reasonable chance of correcting it, in other words, improving efficiency.

In telecommunications, there were two compelling market failures: natural monopoly and the "network externality," each of which received its fair share of regulatory attention.

Traditional Natural Monopoly

Lowry (1973) traces the concept of natural monopoly back to John Stuart Mill in 1848. A natural monopoly occurs in an industry in which the production technology is such that one producer can supply the entire market more cheaply than two or more producers. In such industries, the competitive process will eventually lead to the largest (and therefore cheapest) firm driving all other firms out of the market, thereby monopolizing it through the "natural" outcome of competition. Until recently, it was thought that natural monopoly occurs when the average costs of production declines with increasing volume, although the situation is a bit more complicated in the case of multiproduct firms (Faulhaber 1975). This allows the resulting monopolist to charge prices substantially above costs and cut back the amount supplied and consumed to the profit-maximizing level. More recent work suggests that the mere presence of a cost advantage is not sufficient to enable the monopolist to raise its prices above cost; it appears that only the presence of sunk costs, investments that once made cannot be retrieved for purposes other than the original intent, can deter entry and permit above-cost pricing and monopoly profits (Baumol, Panzar, and Willig 1982).

Nevertheless, the natural monopoly argument is the economic foundation for much of public-utility regulation, and was certainly important in telephone regulation. Indeed, until the late 1960s few questioned that the telephone industry was a natural monopoly. As competition issues heated up in Washington in the early 1970s, it became a fad among regulatory economists to test econometrically whether or not telecommunications was a natural monopoly. Before the various conflicting studies could be resolved, the policy issue was settled: there would be competition. The econometricians moved on to more interesting topics, and by 1980 there were no more studies: the market would decide whether Bell's monopoly was natural or unnatural.

But for a regulated firm believed to be a natural monopoly, the job of the regulator is implicit in the theory: constrain the monopolist from charging above-cost prices and thus force an increase in output and consumption to the point where all resources are efficiently deployed. In the special case where the monopolist produces only one good, economic theory suggests that the regulator must ensure that the price of this good is equal to the marginal cost of producing it—that is, the cost of producing the last unit of that good. If the regulator adheres to this pricing policy, then, in this industry, society's resources will be used at maximum efficiency. How can we know this? Because the only consumers who will buy the good are those who derive a value from consumption at least as great as the price they must pay. If that price is equal to the marginal cost of production, then the resources expended in producing the good or service result in an increase in value for the economy as a whole.

However, this simple theory must be modified if average costs are declining. In a single-product natural monopoly, the cost of producing the last unit is generally less than the average cost. As a result, setting the price at marginal cost will not be sufficient to cover the firm's total costs. In these circumstances, a special variation of the general economic theory of "second-best," suggests that prices be set at average cost (greater than marginal cost), including a cost of capital. However, this "second-best" solution may be improved upon through the use of more sophisticated pricing techniques, such as volume discounts (Faulhaber and Panzar 1977; Willig 1978) and other market-segmentation approaches (such as charging industrial, commercial, and residential customers different rates), that maintain an overall rate level, so that the monopoly earns only a fair return on its investment and no more.

In the case of a multiproduct natural monopoly, such as telecommunications, the job becomes more difficult, conceptually as well as practically. The regulator must still ensure that the monopoly does not earn monopoly profits, but now must oversee the setting of many prices for the firm's many products, some of which may be substitutes for each other (such as private line service and MTS) or complements to each other (such as access and long-distance). The economic theory of "second-best" suggests the use of Ramsey pricing (Baumol and Bradford 1970), wherein those products most responsive to price ("elastic") are priced close to marginal cost, and those products which are least responsive to price ("inelastic") are priced substantially higher than marginal cost. As in the single-product case, the Ramsey method can be extended to include volume-discount pricing and market segment pricing.

In principle, the market-failure/natural-monopoly justification for regulation leads naturally to a regulatory goal: constrain the firm from taking monopoly profits and encourage prices that lead to greater efficiency. The regulatory process itself thus creates another problem: If the firm's profit is forever constrained, then what incentive does it have to minimize costs and make wise investments? The regulator, then, must monitor the firm's productive efficiency as well as its pricing efficiency. Indeed, early theoretical work (Averch and Johnson 1962) seemed to confirm the suspicion that the very process of regulation reduced the regulated firm's incentives to minimize costs.

Cross-subsidy is another concern that pervades multiproduct public utility regulation, as we've seen from our previous discussions of the FCC in the 1970s. Is one group of consumers paying "too much" for its service, while another group pays "too little"? In a natural monopoly where marginal costs are less than average costs, and substantial overhead costs, not economically attributable to any specific service, must be paid by the body of customers as a whole, the meaning of "too much" and "too little" is certainly not obvious. Despite the prevalence of the term in regulatory debate and its use in various economic texts, it was not until 1975 (Faulhaber 1975) that the term "cross-subsidy" was given a precise definition and analysis: if a service, or group of services, pays more than the cost of providing that service (or group of services) on a stand-alone basis, then that (group of) service(s) is providing a subsidy. For example, if long-distance were priced above stand-alone cost (in order that the price of other services could be kept low) so that it was possible for another supplier, using available technology, to provide long-distance more cheaply (while not losing money) without at the same time providing all the other services, such as access, local and long-distance, then long-distance would be providing a subsidy to those other services.

Of course, if subsidies were present in the rate structure of a regulated monopoly, other firms would be attracted to the profit opportunities inherent in cross-subsidies, regardless of whether the subsidies were for "good" social purposes (assuring universal service) or "bad" private purposes (predatory pricing in competitive markets). Therefore, if the regulators permitted entry by competitors, we would expect that the monopoly would adjust its prices to eliminate both "good" and "bad" subsidies. Of course, the regulators need not permit such adjustment; they may wish to continue those subsidies they consider good and even retain some bad subsidies, the elimination of which might discourage entrants whose economic existence depends upon such pricing distortions.

Several surprising conclusions came out of the literature on cross-subsidy and the potential for competitive entry. For example, efficient prices (Ramsey prices) need not be subsidy-free; hence, a regulator successful at directing a monopoly toward the most efficient use of resources may thereby be creating cross-subsidy, thus setting up incentives for competitive entry. Furthermore, there may be no prices that are subsidy-free. Even if the monopolist is efficient and the regulator is squeezing all excess profits out of the rate structure, it may be impossible for total revenues to cover total costs in a way that does not create incentives for others to enter.

Subsequent work in the economics of natural monopoly has focused on entry issues and the sustainability of natural monopoly (Baumol, Panzar, and Willig 1982; Sharkey 1982). These advances in economic thought about natural monopoly were occurring at about the same time that telecommunications regulators were abandoning the natural monopoly concept as an intellectual rationale (honored more in the breach than the observance) for their own activities.

The Network Externality: Universal Service

Natural monopoly was not the only market failure to plague tele-communications. The peculiarly interdependent nature of the demand for telephone service also led to market failure, and, again, regulatory intervention seemed the only solution.

For any individual customer, the value of being linked into the telephone network depends crucially on who else is linked. In the extreme case, a telephone network with one subscriber is absolutely valueless. More realistically, a network that connects 30 percent of U.S. households is less valuable to a subscriber than a network that connects 60 percent. Now, a potential subscriber, deciding whether or not to purchase telephone service, will consider only his or her personal benefit: "Will I get enough value from this service to make it worth paying for?" But others would also benefit should this potential subscriber join—all those individuals who might want to call or be called by this person. For example, suppose our hypothetical subscriber would be willing to pay only $12.00 per month to be on the telephone network, but, collectively, the subscriber's friends, relatives, and, possibly, creditors value his or her availability for calling at $9.00. If the telephone company charges $15.00 per month for subscription, our hypothetical customer would not join, even though his or her personal benefit plus the benefit to potential fellow-communicators is worth $21.00. This potential subscriber is failing to take into account all the social benefits to be derived from his or her subscription. Because some of these benefits are external to the decisionmaker, economists refer to them as "externalities," and this particular demand interdependence is called the "network externality" (Rohlfs 1974).

The network-externality issue was news to economists in the mid-1970s, but it was old hat to telephone regulators and regulatees. They just called it "universal service." Everyone knew, after all, that a telephone system with more people in it was more valuable to each of its members; the social objective of universal service followed from this simple truth. The theory of network externality merely formalized and made analytically tractable a concept familiar to telephone people as far back as Vail.

The economic theory of pricing for a regulated monopoly proved to extend easily to incorporate efficient adjustments for the externality. If some consumers are not taking service because it's too expensive to subscribe, and yet it would be socially beneficial for them to do so, then the price of subscription must be lowered. Access to the network must be subsidized via an increase in rates for other services. In our example above, the telephone company's subscription price must be set below $12.00 per month, even though its cost is higher, if this socially beneficial customer is to join. This artificially low price must then be subsidized by higher rates for, perhaps, long-distance service. In telecommunications, estimates by Rohlfs (1979) suggested that the subsidy of local by toll, via separations and settlements, was in the right direction, if not precisely the correct amount.

This argument assumes, however, that the price of subscription must be the same for everyone; indeed, this conforms with actual practice. This need not be the case. Let's say that, in our example, 90 percent of the potential customers would find that their private benefit from subscription easily exceeded the cost of $15.00. For another 5 percent, the social benefit would exceed $15.00, but the private benefit would not. It is this group that actually requires a subsidy if universal service is to be achieved.[1] To subsidize the subscription price for 95 percent of households when only 5 percent really need it is not only grossly inefficient, it provides incentives for firms to enter the markets that are being used by the monopoly to provide such a substantial subsidy. If the subsidy were more carefully targeted to the marginal 5 percent, such a small amount could be financed entirely by the federal government (much as the CAB handled mail subsidies prior to 1978) or by a small surcharge on long-distance rates. In reality, *every* subscriber has been subsidized by long-distance rates. As a result, the surcharge has been enormous, and firms have flocked to the profit opportunity thereby created.

Yet another dimension to the network-externality/universal-service problem is that certain geographic areas of the country were alleged to be more costly to serve, both for access and for local and long-distance usage. The argument has been made that these areas, primarily rural, need an extra subsidy to ensure that universal service is achieved and maintained. If their cost of service is (to continue our example) $20.00 rather than $15.00, they will need a subsidy of another $5.00 per month, per line, to correct for the network externality. However, the externality argument does not throw out costs altogether. In fact, if costs are higher in rural areas, the proper prices should elicit a higher rate of nonsubscription, all else being equal, than in less costly areas. The network externality need not justify additional subsidies to high-cost areas or high-cost independent companies.

Public Policy and the Public Interest

Having stated the economic case for traditional regulation of telecommunications, we now briefly review how the FCC's performance in the period of regulated monopoly measured up against this public interest rationale. Taking the economic view of the public interest—correcting for market failure—the regulators do not seem to have done a very good job. If the public interest was guiding the decisions of the regulators during the monopoly era, its influence was too subtle for most of us to discern. Still, suppose the market-failure rationale was more than just window dressing for regulation; suppose regulators were actually committed to correcting the market failures of natural monopoly and the network externality. How well did they do?

Productive Efficiency

Correcting market failure implies that regulators must ensure that the regulated monopoly is operating efficiently. Had the regulators been effective, for example, even complete deregulation would have resulted in no changes in the size, composition, or wage rates of the work force or in the nature or amount of investment. However, under even the very incomplete deregulation associated with divestiture, substantial cost reductions have occurred at both AT&T and the BOC's. For instance, the size of the work force at Bell of Pennsylvania decreased from 33,000 at the time of divestiture to 19,400 by mid-1986. Similar improvements have been occurring throughout the old Bell System, hardly evidence that the old regime of regulated monopoly led to efficient operations.

Pricing

Correcting market failures also requires that regulators strive for Ramsey prices. However, telephone prices tended to follow the reverse of the Ramsey rule. Long-distance is a very price-responsive service (Taylor 1980), which therefore should be priced low—it was priced high. Access (subscription) is a price-insensitive service, which should be priced high — it was priced low. Regulators specifically rejected Ramsey pricing, relying instead on accounting allocations of common overhead costs to judge the fairness of prices. Apparently, this approach was used for administrative ease and to eliminate Bell's ability to cross-subsidize. Of course, any relation between assigned costs, allocated by the book, and economic costs is purely coincidental. The use of such accounting procedures for ratemaking assures that prices do not reflect any market factors, *except* as reflected in cost allocations.

Volume Discounts

The use of volume discounts was specifically frowned on by the FCC as a device for price discrimination, forbidden by the Communications Act (which was interpreted to allow differential rates for business and residence, and different markups over cost for urban and rural users). But their usefulness in increasing aggregate efficiency in a regulated monopoly is well-established and clearly recognized, even by the FCC staff (Duvall 1984). However, prohibition on resale, necessary to maintain significant volume discounts, ran counter to the FCC's intention in the late 1970s to use market forces to control Bell's potential for cross-subsidy. The regulators thus faced a conflict between optimal regulated-monopoly pricing and reliance on market forces and competition.

Universal Service: Long-Distance to Access

Since access appeared to have been underpriced according to Ramsey pricing, and long-distance overpriced, it might seem that the regulators had taken seriously the network externality and attempted to correct it by using internal cross-subsidies to keep access rates low. While the general direction of the subsidy supports that view, a closer look at the problem suggests a bleaker conclusion.

As more and more households were added to the network in the postwar era, the private benefit to those who remained unconnected continued to grow. This suggests that the subsidy required to induce people to join the network should have decreased over this period. Instead, it increased very substantially, indicating that the regulators had reasons other than the network externality for continuing the subsidy.

As previously discussed, a much smaller subsidy, aimed at only those potential subscribers who actually needed such inducement to join, would have accomplished the objectives of universal service at perhaps one-tenth the cost of separations and settlements. The use of "telephone stamps," similar to food stamps, has been suggested as one form of a targeted subsidy. That the regulators chose a subsidy so much broader and all-encompassing again suggests that reasons other than universal service lay behind their actions.

Universal Service: Urban to Rural

The use of the network externality to justify extra subsidies to high-cost rural areas and companies is weak indeed. And yet regulators encouraged and defended nationwide averaging of rates and pooling of separations costs, which led to such subsidies. This policy generally favored rural areas and areas served by independents, including the high-growth sunbelt, at the expense of low-cost regions, generally Bell-served, usually urban/suburban, and to some extent low-growth rustbelt. Not only was this policy inefficient because prices were far from economic costs, but it also removed any incentives the high-cost companies might have had to reduce costs. As a result, the system engendered overinvestment in plant and overuse by customers of facilities in subsidized areas.

In general, regulators' attempts to correct the market failures in telecommunications have been unsuccessful. Only the subsidy to encourage universal service appears to have been generally correct, but it was not "target-efficient," nor was it moving in the right direction. While their record is probably no worse than other regulatory commissions, telecommunications regulators failed to correct or even substantially ameliorate the market failures that characterized the industry.

In conclusion, the public interest theory of regulation does not seem to have guided telecommunications regulators during this period. Economic efficiency certainly wasn't being served, and the solution to the network-externality issue was at best extremely inefficient. In Chapter 3, we discussed how economists and political scientists have been developing new theories concerning the behavior of regulators and regulatees, based on interest group politics and access to the regulatory game. This new and more cynical view has all but displaced the more traditional public interest theory, which dates back at least to the 1930s. In this chapter, we have briefly examined the behavior of regulators during the period of regulated monopoly from the point of view of several possible public interest theories, and we have seen that these theories came nowhere near describing what regulators were up to. While this does not mean that the regulatory-game cynics are correct, it certainly does prove that if the public interest view of regulation has any validity at all, it is not in the domain of telecommunications.

The Economics of Antitrust

During the period following the *Carterfone* and the *MCI* decisions, the FCC was most concerned with the possibility of cross-subsidization and predation. The Justice Department joined in that concern in 1974. Since this single issue dominated the policy debates of the 1970s, determining the form of the divestiture decision, we turn now to an exploration of the economics of antitrust – the ability and incentives of a monopolist to engage in anticompetitive and predatory responses to new entrants. In doing so, we take Baxter's point of view (*Wall Street Journal* 1982: 28) – "the sole goal of antitrust is economic efficiency" – rather than the Brandeisian view of Judge Greene – "the philosophy of . . . the antitrust laws, of effective controls to make sure that a bigger corporation will not overwhelm the interest of the smaller competitors and of the public" (*Telecommunications Reports* 1986).

As summarized in Brennan (1986), three economic concerns motivated Justice's case (and presumably the regulators' efforts):

1. The monopolist (Bell) would use its monopoly power in one market (access) to subsidize below-cost predatory pricing in competitive markets, in order to throttle competition;
2. The monopolist would use its unregulated equipment supplier (Western Electric) to overcharge its captive regulated customers (the BOC's), thus realizing profits that would otherwise be regulated away in the BOC's; and
3. The regulated monopolist would deny interconnection with a needed bottleneck facility (access) to competitors attempting to enter a market (long-distance or CPE) otherwise competitive, but which required the joint use of the monopoly-owned bottleneck.

We will discuss each allegation in turn, concentrating not on a monopolist's *ability* to so act, but rather on the *incentive* of the rational profit-maximizing monopolist to do so.

Subsidizing Predatory Pricing

Suppose the king of Economia had been gracious enough to grant you the state monopoly on the sale of coffee throughout his royal domain. You had taken advantage of this position to expand into the supply of cream and sugar, convincing the king that the provision of these goods should also be your monopoly. Lately, though, the Royal Person has had second thoughts and has permitted competitive entry into the markets for cream and sugar. Your product managers in each of these markets are panicky, anticipating vigorous entry by other suppliers, with a concomitant loss of market share. They suggest to you that they be permitted to lower their prices below the marginal cost to supply these goods, in order to drive out the new entrants and remonopolize these markets—a permissible strategy here in Economia, though not in the United States. They also suggest that you raise the price of coffee, your remaining monopoly, to finance the temporary below-cost pricing in the other markets. Would you take their advice?

You realize that your product managers' predatory strategy consists of two rather separate propositions: (1) losing money today (below-cost pricing) in the hope of driving competitors out of the cream and sugar markets so that you can raise your prices back to the monopoly level at some future point (recoupment); and (2) making up the short-term losses by raising prices in the monopoly coffee market. The major component of the strategy is (1), which, like any investment, requires you to spend money today in hope of a greater return tomorrow, and which, like any investment, may or may not be profitable. Item (2) is simply a financing strategy, which has some flaws. First, since you are a canny monopolist, you have already set the price for coffee at the profit-maximizing level; increasing it beyond that will only result in losing money—decreased demand would more than offset any profits derived from the increase in price. Therefore, any financing of (1) must come from existing coffee profits.

The second flaw is that if (1) is a good idea, a profitable investment, you will be able to find financing for it whether or not you happen to control the coffee monopoly. If it is a good investment, then perhaps you and your stockholders will choose to retain the coffee profits to finance predatory pricing in cream and sugar. However, even if you did not happen to have a coffee monopoly, you would still be able to raise the money in the capital markets to finance your investment in predation. In other words, the fact that you control the coffee monopoly does not increase or decrease the attractiveness of your potential predation investment, nor does it make it easier or harder for you to finance it. Profitable investments, if in fact predation be profitable, will always find willing investors, either within the firm (retained earnings or depreciation funds) or outside the firm (debt or equity). The presence or absence of a monopoly market and a competitive market within the same firm is simply irrelevant.

All of which means you can focus your full attention on your subordinates' predation strategy; is it a good investment for you and your stockholders? Obviously, the success of the strategy depends crucially on recoupment. If your tough-guy stance does not scare off competitors so that you can later have the market to yourself, you can never cash in on your investment. All you will have done is lose money for your stockholders. Since the profitability of this strategy hinges on recoupment, and recoupment hinges on scaring off competitors, what are the factors you must consider?

If you find this market attractive enough to lose money in order to keep it in the long run, so will your competitors. Though they may be smaller than you, what counts is the investment resources that they can draw upon to finance a price war. If the cream and sugar markets are really attractive, your competitors may have access to enough venture capital to outlast you, no matter what their size.

The competitors you face in these markets today are not the only potential competitors. Even if you drive today's entrants from the field, there are others waiting in the wings, who know that your stockholders are unwilling to lose money forever and that you will eventually have to accommodate to entry.[2]

For predation to be a profitable strategy, then, you would want to make sure that:

1. Your competitors today are likely to be the only competitors who could even enter. If there are lots of potential entrants, perhaps from other countries, just waiting to take you on, you may be seeing losses for a long time to come;
2. Your competitors, both actual and potential, are much smaller than your firm, with limited internal resources;
3. Your competitors, both actual and potential, do not have access to venture capital or other means of financing an extended price war for control of the market; and
4. The strategy does not expose you to the risk of treble damages in antitrust court, as is the case in the U.S.

No doubt there are markets in which these conditions obtain, and, in such markets, predatory pricing would be a real problem. However, these are rather special conditions, and unless they all hold, predation is unlikely to be a profitable strategy. It would appear that the problem may not be widespread and certainly not as ubiquitous as is popularly believed.

Applying this scenario to telecommunications, access would be the coffee monopoly, CPE would be the sugar market, and long-distance the cream market. Would we believe predatory pricing in CPE and long-distance to be a rational strategy for the old Bell System? If Bell's managers believed that there were only a few small radio suppliers who could sell microwave systems to private customers or that MCI was the only firm willing to supply private line services, then predation might have looked good. While this short-sighted attitude may have prevailed in 1960, just after the *Above 890* decision, and perhaps even as late as the 1969 *MCI* decision, by the early 1970s the prospect of entry by American, Canadian, and Japanese electronics firms into CPE, and IBM and other large firms into long-distance must have been evident even to monopoly-conditioned Bell executives. While it is conceivable (though by no means at all certain) that TELPAK was launched as a predatory pricing vehicle in 1960, it is extremely unlikely that price responses by Bell were designed to lose money against a formidable array of actual and potential competitors.

However, the cross-subsidy and predation accusations against the old Bell System focused on the fact that Bell was a regulated monopoly. While predation might be relatively rare for an unregulated monopoly (as we have just argued), there are special incentives for a regulatee to engage in such activities. Returning to the land of Economia, suppose that the king himself determined what price you were permitted to charge for coffee, based on the cost of producing and distributing the product. However, should you undertake predation in the cream and sugar markets, you would be able to allocate some of the cream and sugar production costs to coffee, pretending to the king that these were properly assigned to the monopoly and should be recovered in the coffee rates. Using this ruse, you would be able to raise the price of coffee and drop the prices of cream and sugar, thus financing without loss predatory activities in potentially competitive markets.

The flaw in this argument is the assumption that, not only can you fool the king with this cost-allocation hanky-panky, but this is the *only* way you can fool him into letting you raise the price of coffee. It is possible that a regulator, who cannot be expected to know every single management detail, could fall for the shell game of cost allocation. However, this is by no means the only shell game, and if a regulator can't detect cost misallocations, then it follows that he or she also can't detect: higher than normal salaries for executives; greater than normal executive perquisites, such as corporate helicopters, lush offices designed by leading architects, etc.; extra staff to supervise, expanding management's responsibilities; higher wages for workers; and greater benefits for all employees.

Clearly, these stratagems do not lead to higher profits for the regulated firm's shareholders (which would be easy for the regulator to detect) but to inefficiencies in operations and higher returns to executives, workers, and perhaps favored suppliers (which are hard to detect). The king always knows less about your coffee business than you do—after all, he has wars to fight and taxes to collect. You hardly need to misallocate costs to your coffee monopoly when there are so many other ways to justify rate hikes.

All of these shell games, if undetectable by regulators, could seem to justify increasing the price of coffee, probably up to its monopoly level. If your coffee firm can achieve the monopoly price without resorting to cost misallocation for predatory purposes, using one of the 999 other ways to fool the regulator, then you are not effectively regulated at all, and the previous analysis is still valid: predation is unlikely to be profitable.[3]

The argument that regulation makes the cross-subsidy/predation strategy profitable depends utterly on the firm's assumed ability to fool the regulator; it founders on the logical extension of this assumption. As long as cost misallocations are not the only way the regulator can be fooled, then this monopoly is regulated in name only, and cross-subsidy and predation are no more attractive than they would be to an unregulated monopoly.

However, the argument that regulation makes cross-subsidy and predation much more likely is disturbing at a more profound level. If true, the obvious remedy is to get rid of regulation, not to "fix" the regulatee. If regulation is there to correct for a market failure, but actually causes new problems to arise, then we obviously need to get rid of regulation and find a new way to correct the alleged failure. In Chapter 5, we noted that analysts close to the AT&T antitrust case joked that the FCC was the unindicted co-conspirator; if the law had permitted it, might they not have sought "divestiture" of the FCC as well as (or perhaps instead of) AT&T?

The Captive Supplier

Back in Economia, you have convinced your king that, in order to guarantee a secure source of coffee for the inhabitants of his realm, you must buy a coffee plantation, even though the growing of coffee is a competitive industry. Would you find it profitable to sell your own beans to your own coffee monopoly at a price above the competitive level? You are currently making all the profits that the Economia coffee market will bear. Raising the price of inputs (beans) may transfer part of those profits to the upstream subsidiary (the plantation), but does not increase (or diminish) them one iota.

However, the argument goes, if your monopoly is regulated by the king so that the price of a cup of coffee is based strictly on cost, then raising the price of beans would enable you to convince the king that your costs had risen, and so, too, should your coffee rates. By manipulating the price of beans, you could fool the king into permitting you to raise your rates for coffee to the monopoly level, thus using your vertical integration to evade the king's monopoly-profit constraint.

This is exactly the same argument used to suggest that regulation increases the risk of cross-subsidy and predation: The regulated monopoly can fool the regulator into permitting the firm to increase price to the monopoly level via some cost hanky-panky, in this case by manipulation of the upstream firm's transfer price. The counterargument is also the same: if the regulator can be duped on transfer prices, then he or she can no doubt be fooled in a thousand other ways as well. Provided the firm has at least one other regulatory cost scam in its bag of tricks, then this vertical transfer-pricing scheme is unnecessary and irrelevant. The firm will already be charging the monopoly price and will be uninterested in moving profits around among subsidiaries for no apparent reason.

Again, the most disturbing aspect of this argument is that its validity depends on the presence of regulation. And again, if it is true, isn't the obvious solution to get rid of regulation? The more closely we look at regulation, the less it seems the solution and the more it seems the problem.

Refusal to Deal

Again we travel to the land of Economia to see how your coffee monopoly is doing. A number of new entrants are supplying cream and sugar to your customers. Your still-panicky product managers, piqued at your wise refusal to price below cost to save their market share, now insist that you do not permit your customers to use any cream or sugar in your coffee except your own subsidiary's.

For once, your product managers make sense. Since in Economia cream and sugar are only employed to flavor coffee, your competitors' products are useless if customers cannot put them in your coffee. By refusing to permit your competitors' products in your coffee, you are able to extend your effective monopoly to include the cream and sugar markets and to realize extra profits from charging monopoly prices for these products. Instead of charging what the cream and sugar cost you, $0.05 per serving of each, you can now charge $0.10 per serving of each. Whether or not you are regulated, this sounds like a profitable proposition, so you follow your product managers' suggestion.

Now the king can obviously see what's going on here (he'll not be fooled by outright refusals to deal) and makes it clear that he believes you are thwarting his desire for competition in the cream and sugar markets. You tell him that you are willing to accommodate the new competitors, but, of course, you must protect the consumers. Consequently, it is necessary to impose a requirement that, whenever a customer wants to put a serving of a competitor's sugar in his or her coffee, this can only be done through a "sweetening arrangement," obtainable from you for a fee of $0.05. In addition, for every serving of cream sold to a customer, your competitor must pay you a "coffee-access charge" of $0.05. As long as you are actually able to collect these charges, you really don't care how much of the market your competitors take from you, because, either way, you make a nickel profit on every serving sold in the market, both yours and theirs.

Furthermore, any form of price control—cost-based regulation or otherwise—in the monopoly coffee market will only be partially effective. Suppose that some form of price regulation successfully reduces the price of black coffee from its monopoly level of $1.00 to $0.50. Drinkers of black coffee will receive the full benefit of this price reduction, but those who prefer cream and sugar can still be forced to pay the monopoly price of $1.20 ($1.00 for coffee + $0.10 for cream + $0.10 for sugar) by the simple stratagem of raising your subsidiary's cream and sugar prices to $0.35 per serving of each, and your fees for the use of competitors' products to $0.30 per serving of each.

In short, refusing to permit use of complementary products with your monopoly products gives you a very powerful tool with which to reap excess profits in markets other than your basic monopoly markets. A monopolist, whether regulated or not, would find it advantageous to use that tool, provided the risk of successful antitrust prosecution did not outweigh the profit benefits.

Applying these lessons to telecommunications, we see we have arrived at the economic heart of Justice's case against AT&T. The cross-subsidy/predation charge and the charge of hiding profits in the upstream supplier appear very weak. The profit motive just wasn't there for the Bell System to take such risk. However, the vertical-foreclosure charge—of refusing to provide access lines for competitors' long-distance service, of refusing to permit interconnection of competitors' CPE—must be taken very seriously. Clearly, the Bell System would have had plenty of profit motive, and its actions on access charges for long-distance and connecting devices for CPE are consistent with this profit-motive pattern.

Of course, Bell's story was also consistent with its actions. Bell wanted to protect universal service; when that goal was placed in jeopardy by competition, it looked for ways to make competition work while still maintaining a commitment to end-to-end universal service. When CPE was opened to competition by *Carterfone*, Bell sought only to protect the network against spurious signals and voltages. When switched long-distance was opened to competition by *Execunet*, it sought only to replace the access subsidy, threatened by competition, with the new access charges. But throughout the period regulation was effective in holding profits far below monopoly levels. In responding to competition with aggressive actions, Bell was simply ensuring its own survival, not protecting monopoly profits.

Which of the two models—profit-seeking monopolist or champion of universal service—is closer to the truth, we shall never know. The inability to determine costs empirically, our ignorance about the efficiency or inefficiency of regulated company operations, and a host of other unobservables make it virtually impossible to determine on the basis of market facts if Bell played fair or foul. Without a firm base of facts, we have only our judgment of the players and the play with which to form opinions about Bell's actual behavior:

Bell's aggressive TELPAK response to the *Above 890* decision was likely intended to establish a predatory tough-guy reputation with potential entrants, at a time when Bell thought this would be a small, easily managed problem. Call this likely predation.

Bell's initial refusal to permit interconnection of competitors' CPE and later insistence on the use of a connecting device to protect against "harms to the network" seems to fit well into the refusal-to-deal model. During the late 1960s and early 1970s, when the regulatory battles over interconnection were raging, a substantial number of technical people of my acquaintance at Bell Labs believed "harms to the network" to be a bogus issue, in that it could easily be solved with interconnection standards. In retrospect, it is difficult to imagine how it could have been taken so seriously. Call this refusal to deal.

After Bell was instructed by the FCC to provide access lines for MCI's private line service in the early to mid-1970s, its compliance was grudging and minimal. While Bell's foot-dragging was never a major market factor, it provided plenty of ammunition for the forthcoming Justice and private antitrust suits. Call this a partial and relatively unsuccessful refusal to deal.

After *Execunet* opened up switched entry, Bell attempted to impose the ENFIA access charge to replace the local subsidy that would not be paid by competitive long-distance. Although this is suggestive of refusal to deal, the fact that at divestiture Bell was willing to impose full access charges on itself suggests this really was a subsidy-preserving measure. Had Bell assiduously pursued access charges for its long-distance competitors as part of a refusal-to-deal strategy, it would have attempted to impose an ENFIA-like charge on the competitive carriers when they were still limited to private line service (1972–1978), even though Bell's private line services carry no subsidy surcharge. Instead, it only sought to impose the access charge when the competitive carriers could compete directly with MTS and WATS, which did carry the subsidy burden. Yes, long-distance profits were being protected, but those profits had been earmarked by regulation to subsidize access. Do not call this refusal to deal.

Had Bell's access charges been purely a monopoly-pricing ploy, AT&T would not have so readily acceded to separations-based access charges at the time of divestiture. If such access charges had merely been a means for the local operating subsidiaries of the old Bell System to tap into long-distance profits for the aggrandizement of shareholders or management, AT&T would have been most reluctant to let such a rich lode of profit be divested. Instead, it would have argued at divestiture, as eloquently as MCI had during the ENFIA negotiations, that access charges were mere tribute to the BOC's, and it wanted them reduced. If AT&T knew that such profits were not going to enrich shareholders or management, but rather to reduce subscription rates, then it would readily acquiesce to separations-based access charges. Since that's what it did (rather than complain loudly), do not call this refusal to deal.

Did all of the antitrust accusations against Bell of anticompetitive behavior make sense? No—while Bell had the *ability* to do everything of which it was accused, it only had a strong *motivation* to refuse to deal. Was there any antitrust, anticompetitive risk at all? Yes, indeed—refusal to deal is a strategy at once profitable for the monopolist, regulated or not, and damaging to both potential competitors and the consuming public. Did the divestiture reduce this risk of anticompetitive behavior? Yes—by mandating the specific terms of equal access, the MFJ made it tough for the BOC's to deny access, just as the FCC's registration program for CPE made it tough for the Bell System to refuse to interconnect. And no—the incentive to deny access is still there; Judge Greene put enough competitive businesses in the BOC's (Yellow Pages, for one) that, could they find a way to extend their market power by refusing to deal, they no doubt would. However, the rules on access at least appear tight enough to preclude the rather open refusals to deal that occurred during the 1970s in the old Bell System.

Notes

1. The remaining 5 percent do not find sufficient value in communicating via telephone, nor do others find value in being able to communicate with them. Whether these individuals deserve our pity or our envy is beyond the scope of this work to judge; the economists' view is that society can expend its resources in more beneficial ways than thrusting telephones into reluctant hands.
2. Recent theoretical literature by Kreps and Wilson (1982) and Milgrom and Roberts (1982), among many others, has examined the issue of predation in a multiperiod context, where entrants can be driven out in one period if the incumbent is predatory. If the incumbent can establish a reputation for being a tough guy, further entry may be discouraged but not prevented. Eventually, the rational incumbent accommodates to new entry. These models depend on a belief in the possible irrationality of incumbents as well as on entrants having only limited resources available to resist predation. Even using these assumptions that tend to make predation look profitable, the models suggest that predation is not a very robust strategy.
3. If the regulator can only be fooled on a small scale, the firm may need to use all of its thousand ways of cheating to achieve the monopoly price. In this case, denying the firm the ability to play cost allocation games would result in only the most marginal improvement.

References

Averch, H., and L. Johnson. 1962. "Behavior of the Firm Under Regulatory Constraints." *American Economic Review* 52 (December): 1052–1063.

Baumol, W.J., and D.E. Bradford. 1970. "Optimal Departures from Marginal Cost Pricing." *American Economic Review* 70 (June): 265–283.

Baumol, W.J., J.C. Panzar, and R.D. Willig. 1982. *Contestable Markets and the Theory of Industry Structure.* New York: Harcourt Brace Jovanovich, Inc.

Brennan, T. 1986. "Regulated Firms in Unregulated Markets: Understanding the Divestiture in *U.S. vs. AT&T.*" EAG Discussion Paper 86-5, Antitrust Division, U.S. Department of Justice, Washington, D.C.

Duvall, J.B. 1984. "Telephone Rates and Rate Structures: A Regulatory Perspective." In *Telecommunications Access and Public Policy,* edited by M.A. Baughcum and G.R. Faulhaber, pp. 166–204. Norwood, N.J.: Ablex Publishing.

Faulhaber, G.R. 1975. "Cross-subsidization: Pricing in Public Enterprise." *American Economic Review* 65 (December): 966–977.

Faulhaber, G.R., and J.C. Panzar. 1977. "Optimal Two-Part Tariffs with Self-Selection." Bell Laboratories Economic Discussion Paper 74, January.

Kahn, Alfred E. 1984. "The Regulatory Agenda." In *Telecommunications Access and Public Policy,* edited by M.A. Baughcum and G.R. Faulhaber, p. 206. Norwood, N.J.: Ablex Publishing.

Kreps, D., and R. Wilson. 1982. "Reputation and Imperfect Information." *Journal of Economic Theory* 27: 253–279.

Lowry, E.D. 1973. "Justification for Regulation: The Case for Natural Monopoly." *Public Utilities Fortnightly* 92 (November 8): 17–23.

Milgrom, P., and J. Roberts. 1982. "Predation, Reputation, and Entry Deterrence." *Journal of Economic Theory* 27: 280–312.

Rohlfs, J.H. 1974. "A Theory of Interdependent Demand for a Communications Service." *Bell Journal of Economics and Management Science* 5 (Spring): 16–37.

———. 1979. "Economically Efficient Bell System Pricing." Bell Laboratories Economics Discussion Paper 138.

Sharkey, W.W. 1982. *The Theory of Natural Monopoly.* New York: Cambridge University Press.

Taylor, L. 1980. *Telecommunications Demand: A Survey and Critique.* Cambridge, Mass.: Ballinger.

Telecommunications Reports. 1986. June 9, p. 5.

Wall Street Journal. 1982. "A Talk With Antitrust Chief William Baxter." March 4, p. 28.

Willig, R.D. 1978. "Pareto Superiority of Nonlinear Outlay Schedules." *Bell Journal of Economics* 9: 56–69.

CHAPTER 7

Life After Divestiture:
Facing the Future

On January 1, 1984, the divestiture came to pass, and the Bell System was no more. Seven regional holding companies, the trimmed-down AT&T, and a host of competitors were shoved from the nest of regulated monopoly into the crazy-quilt world of Judge Greene's personalized MFJ. Although confident—and contradictory—predictions were made by financial analysts, AT&T and BOC spokespersons, Justice Department and regulatory economists, and academics of every stripe, absolutely no one had the slightest idea of what was going on.

Beyond the tumult and the hype, however, some basic facts would determine the shape of things to come:

The economics of this industry were undergoing radical change: the markets, the services and products, and the technologies. This process had begun long before divestiture and would hold the industry in thrall for long afterward.

All long-distance carriers would have equal access to their customers, under terms and conditions to be embodied in the FCC's access charge. The days of denying competitors the bottleneck facility were over; the days of subsidy to the access line, in the form of inflated carrier-access charges, were not.

Competition would be the reigning political and regulatory *zeitgeist*. Virtually all parties in the industry, including the descendants of the Bell System, declared themselves in favor of more competition. Only some state regulators and rural congressmen, holding out for continued subsidies to their constituents, persisted in saluting the tattered flag of universal service.

Regulation would continue in full force, despite the popular impression that the industry had been deregulated. In fact, a new and powerful regulator, Judge Greene, had muscled his way onto the regulatory scene. The players had multiplied as well—overnight, the seven regional holding companies became important players in the game.

To explore this postdivestiture world, we first examine the industry's competitive situation, focusing on the long-term trends in major markets. Next, we look at the role played by the descendants of the Bell System in these markets and the changes these firms are undergoing because of divestiture. We conclude with a careful look at the regulatory process since divestiture: What are the new battlegrounds? What are the prospects for deregulation and the emergence of a truly competitive marketplace? How have the structural solutions of the late 1970s and early 1980s fared in the real world?

The Struggle for the Market

The first and most obvious effect of divestiture on telecommunications consumers was that they could no longer buy telephone service from a single vendor. Consumers could get their CPE from the local telephone store, their long-distance from AT&T or any of the competitive carriers, and their access and local calling from their local BOC or independent. Trouble was, many customers didn't know and didn't care about these options; what they wanted was telephone service, just like they used to get from the telephone company. Only the very largest institutional customers, such as the Defense Department, General Electric, and IBM, were accustomed to buying their communications systems on a piece-by-piece basis. Most customers had counted on the telephone company to select the right pieces for them and put them together so they worked and stayed working.

The divestiture made that sort of one-stop shopping a thing of the past, but many customers still wanted it. Every firm in the telecommunications market wanted to present itself to the customer as "your systems vendor," the company that could put it all together for them, just like the old telephone company, only better. For example, a manufacturer of PBX's would not want to sell only a PBX to a corporate customer, but would also hope to resell another manufacturer's telephone sets, arrange for enough local access lines, resell the long-distance service of one of the competitive carriers, and provide overall system integration and maintenance. Although the firm actually produces only one part of the total telecommunications system, it can add great value to its service by pulling together all the components from different vendors into a system designed for its customer. In fact, the added value of system integration was believed to be the most profitable part of this new market.

The obvious candidates to handle the customer's systems integration were constrained from doing so by either the MFJ or the FCC's rules. AT&T–Information Systems, the CPE and enhanced-services vendor, could not jointly market and sell with AT&T-Communications, the long-distance vendor, under the FCC's *Second Computer Inquiry* rules.[1] The BOC's were strictly enjoined from the sale of inter-LATA long-distance service and even from making an official recommendation to its customers regarding which carrier was best.

None of the new competitors, either long-distance carriers or CPE suppliers, proved to have the credibility or capability to be a systems vendor across a broad segment of the market. Telecommunications consultants sprang up to meet this need, although the market for systems integrators—firms who purport to make the right choices and put together the right system for the business customer—is somewhat fragmented and oriented to specific market niches. In this regard, it is similar to the computer market, where medium to small firms are often served by custom-software vendors who act as distributors for computer and peripheral-equipment manufacturers. However, IBM is the obvious heavyweight in this market, a role that a more integrated AT&T or BOC could play in telecommunications were it not forbidden to do so.

These two markets, computers and communications, share more than common characteristics—they no doubt share a common future. The underlying technology of both is the same, and the products of each can perform many of the services of the other. Computers can switch phone calls, and PBX's can do computing. Industry analysts predict a day, perhaps five or ten years away, when systems integration for the business customer will include not only telephone service but word processing, commercial data processing, and facsimile and data transmission. The engineers assure us that the technology is there, but will it be put to use? Only if the customer wants it and is willing to pay for it.

Access to most customer groups by competitors new and old has been far superior to predivestiture days. Only the average residential user, a target for both home CPE vendors and long-distance companies, has been reluctant to spend time learning about services and features that are relatively unimportant in his or her life. The implementation of equal access by the BOC's has required that each long-distance consumer, no matter how little they consume, choose (or be assigned) a primary long-distance carrier for "Dial 1" service. For each exchange area, conversion of the local switch to equal access brought an "election day," when customers had to choose their "Dial 1" carrier, a decision that could later be changed, but at some cost. Despite heavy television and print advertising by AT&T and MCI, 30 percent of the customers failed to make a choice, which seems to indicate confusion, ignorance, or lack of interest.[2] Aside from this apathy, however, competitors had little trouble getting in the door to sell their wares. As the BOC's complete their conversions of exchanges to equal access, virtually all of their customers will be accessible to all long-distance carriers.[3]

Long-Distance

In long-distance service, AT&T-Communications has been far better than expected at marketing its wares. Traditionally operations- and engineering-oriented, the predivestiture AT&T Long Lines organization had strongly resisted the corporate shift toward marketing. With the entire long-distance market up for grabs on "election day," the postdivestiture AT&T-Communications applied its considerable reserves of strength to convince most customers to choose them. Surprisingly, they simply outmarketed and outsold the competitive carriers, of which only MCI made a serious showing. By September 1, 1986, 80 percent of the customers had chosen AT&T as their carrier, compared to 10 percent who had chosen MCI and 4 percent Sprint. It is estimated that AT&T will in the end carry off 81 percent of long-distance revenues, MCI 8 percent, and Sprint 4 percent (Rudolph 1986).

As equal access became a reality, the FCC's access charge forced all long-distance carriers to pay the same fees to the BOC's for access. The ENFIA discount for unequal access was gone, and the competitive carriers found themselves in trouble. MCI, the most successful of the new competitors, saw its return on equity nose-dive from its 1979–1984 average of 125.3 percent to 9.8 percent in 1985 (Hayes 1986). Further, the FCC introduced a subscriber line charge of $2.00 per month, levied on all subscribers, to help defray that portion of subscriber access lines allocated by regulatory fiat to interstate service. This shifted the recovery of this cost away from carriers and onto subscribers. As a result, AT&T was able to reduce its long-distance rates by a significant 22 percent between 1984 and 1986. The long-term prospect is that all such costs will be removed from the carriers and their long-distance rates, to be recovered from customers, through their subscriber line charges. However, this transition from subsidy to cost-based pricing will be lengthy.

Long-distance resellers, whose economic existence depended on their ability to arbitrage AT&T's rate schedule between MTS and WATS, found their profit margins squeezed from 30 percent to zero as AT&T, with the FCC's strong urging, moved its tariffed rates closer to costs. Their numbers were reduced from around 500 in 1984 to less than 300 at the end of 1985 (Wilke 1985).

The BOC's are obvious potential competitors in the long-distance market. Already they carry a substantial amount of toll traffic (intra-LATA), and in some states intra-LATA competition is prohibited by the state commission. The BOC's have the facilities in place to offer inter-LATA long-distance almost immediately and have strongly protested their continuing exclusion from this market by the MFJ (Maremont 1985).

Even without using their own facilities, the BOC's could deploy, were it not prohibited, a "least-cost long-distance" service, whereby a customer's long-distance call would be sent over the long-distance carrier that offered the cheapest rate for that call at that specific time. The customer would be relieved of the need to choose a long-distance carrier separate from his local telephone company and would know that each call was placed at the least possible cost. The long-distance carriers would lose any market presence with the customer, becoming merely wholesalers of long-distance transmission to the BOC. Of course, such a service would violate the MFJ provisions enjoining the BOC's from long-distance and mandating equal access, since only the BOC could offer such an interexchange service.

Competitive Prospects

While long-distance has all the attributes of a competitive service (plenty of excess capacity, free entry and exit), it appears that AT&T-Communications will continue to dominate this market, simply because it is better than any of the other carriers at serving the customer. There are others who could give AT&T a serious tussle: the BOC's, for example, and perhaps IBM. The BOC's, of course, are not permitted in this market, and IBM has made it clear that it will keep away from any market in which it could be regulated. Until MFJ and FCC regulation is removed, AT&T apparently will not have to face a varsity-class competitor.

Access and Local Service

In the general access and local service market, the BOC's maintain an almost 100 percent market share—what firm can compete against a heavily subsidized service? However, the threat of bypass competition for the local loop looms large. Though the FCC is slowly decreasing the subsidy element in carrier-access charges, heavy toll users still pay a price substantially above cost for long-distance service that traverses BOC facilities. Customers who can find alternative means of access to long-distance carriers receive substantially lower long-distance rates, justifying the expense of such bypass facilities.

One alternative means of access is provided by suppliers of shared tenant services (STS). These suppliers have opened up a new market, providing a broad array of telecommunications services to office buildings, condominiums, and office parks, including telephone, cable TV, intercom, security services, and even long-distance. Typically, the developer of the building complex wires the premises, provides a PBX, and runs access lines from the PBX to the local BOC. The STS operators have the ability to bypass the local BOC access facilities and take their subscribers' toll traffic straight to a long-distance carrier, thereby avoiding access charges and the subsidy therein.[4]

From the perspective of the BOC's, it is not yet clear whether these operators are mini-operating companies, competitors, potential distributors of BOC services, or potential customers of BOC skills, such as building wiring. STS operators are forcing the BOC's to rethink their approach to their markets of geographically concentrated customers.

Wenders (1986) argues persuasively that STS entry is a legitimate competitive response to the changing cost pattern of local exchange. Years ago, when local loops were relatively cheap and exchange switching was relatively expensive, the least-cost network used few switches and long loops from the central switch to subscribers. A town of 20,000 people might have had one central telephone office, with subscribers from all over town connected to that one switch by local loops. Since this was the least-cost design at the time, the telephone company laid out its network accordingly.

Since then, loops have become relatively more expensive than switching, and optimal system design today would call for more switches and shorter loops. For example, our town of 20,000 might use two or three central offices, each serving fewer subscribers with shorter loops. However, the local BOC network reflects the older design. STS vendors are adapting the design of the older network to today's economics. For an office park, the STS system provides much shorter loops, reaching only the operator's PBX on the park's premises, and then transports calls from the office park to the BOC switch via PBX trunk circuits. In this way, an office park with, say, 3,000 telephones will have 3,000 connections, averaging 1,000 feet in length, to the park's PBX, and perhaps 100 connections running the 5,000 feet from the PBX to the BOC's central switch. Under the old system, 3,000 connections averaging 5,000 feet in length would run from each phone to the BOC's switch. In Wenders' view, STS operators are moving the system toward a more efficient design.

Others see STS as a marginal business opportunity. Medium to large businesses find it cost effective to install their own PBX and communication systems, so the STS operator has little to offer them. Thus restricted to buildings and office parks catering to small businesses, the STS operator must invest heavily in electronic gear and building wiring and then compete with the local telephone company's subsidized exchange rates to attract customers. Though the STS operator can offer services such as an integrated computing facility and data network that the local telephone company cannot, customers often are concerned about the security of their data in such shared arrangements. However, as local exchange rates increase toward costs, the prospects for STS may improve.

The most obvious potential competitor in local access is AT&T. Direct connection with its customers would not only permit AT&T (or any carrier, for that matter) to avoid the access charge but also improve AT&T's ability to serve as a system vendor. However, AT&T has been extremely cautious about approaching the local access business for fear of being accused of undoing the divestiture and remonopolizing the business. Bradley O'Brien of Perspective Telecommunications Group is no doubt correct in his assessment of the situation: "If AT&T bypasses, it'll bring down the hammers of hell." Even so, AT&T offered Megacom service, which permits their WATS customers to connect directly to them (Maremont 1986).

Another source of competition in local exchange has been the coin-phone market, one in which AT&T and others have been quite aggressive. In many states, BOC's have been required to provide interconnection with non-BOC pay phones, which means that manufacturers can sell their phones to gas stations, corner stores, shopping malls and airport operators. Their sales pitch: the operator gets to keep more of the money in the box than from a BOC coin phone.

Competitive Prospects

Local access continues to be a market requiring huge sunk investment. The potential for competition for institutions and large agglomerations of businesses and residences is promising, but competition for the standard single-line household or small business is unlikely to materialize with available technologies. Cellular radio, the technology underlying the new mobile-phone systems, shows some possibility of filling this gap. However, in its present incarnation, it simply does not deliver sufficient capacity to be a serious competitor for the local loop in most markets.

Customer Premises Equipment

In business CPE, AT&T and the BOC's are recovering from the significant loss of market that characterized the period immediately after the FCC's registration program went into effect. In preparation for divestiture, AT&T took over CPE marketing and sales operations from the BOC's in 1983, and it was a disaster. Noncarrier distributors captured 48 percent of the market, leaving Bell with less than 45 percent (with the remainder supplied by independent telephone companies). Since then, the regional holding companies, permitted to sell but not manufacture CPE,[5] have gone from no market share at divestiture to 8 percent in 1985 (Wilke 1985), and the share of the independent distributors has declined by a like amount over that period. AT&T–Information Systems has stabilized its falling market share by extreme price-cutting, but as a consequence its profit margins have been badly squeezed.

AT&T-IS's efforts to expand its product portfolio from PBX and key systems into computers has had mixed success; their own 3B line of processors was an embarrassment, but the Olivetti-produced AT&T PC6300 personal computer has been a modest yet solid success. Time will tell if this integration of computers and telecommunications sales and marketing is the direction of the future for the CPE business.

Competitive Prospects

The CPE market continues to be highly competitive, but the easy pickings early entrants could count on because of Bell's clumsy product development and sales efforts are no more. AT&T has turned in an overall substandard performance in this market, although they have done reasonably well in certain submarkets. The complete absence of sunk costs and other barriers to entry assure the consumer and policymaker alike that competition will continue to provide innovative, least-cost CPE to consumers.

Service Provider Equipment

Western Electric, AT&T's manufacturing subsidiary, has loomed large in both of the Justice Department's antitrust suits against Bell, accused of overpricing the switching, transmission, and other gear it sold to the operating companies (see Chapter 6). Now that the BOC's are free to purchase their equipment from any supplier, how has Western fared?

Western Electric, reorganized several times since divestiture, with the "Western" name now consigned to history, has successfully kept its BOC customers for large switching systems and basic transmission gear, principally because of its strong reputation for after-market service. It has not done as well in supplying the BOC's with PBX's and key systems, and it is only one of many suppliers of new fiber-optic transmission systems. Twice, AT&T has paid a high price to retain its manufacturing capability, believing that vertical integration would be a crucial asset in the coming competitive wars. As yet, Western Electric and its organizational descendants are far from justifying that price.

Competitive Prospects

Manufacturing the large systems needed by telephone companies has become a highly competitive business, both domestically and worldwide. AT&T has strong and determined rivals for its domestic market, including GTE, IT&T, France's CIT-Alcatel, Sweden's Ericcson, Britain's Stromberg-Carlson, Germany's Siemens, Japan's NEC, and Canada's Northern Telecom, the last having a 37 percent share of the U.S. market (Mason and Maremont 1985). After a slow start overseas, AT&T is expecting to capture a significant piece of the French switch market through its joint venture with Philips, the Dutch electronics giant.

The Children of Divestiture

In Chapter 5, we noted the outpouring of sympathy for the soon-to-be-independent operating companies immediately after the divestiture announcement, feelings apparently shared by Judge Greene as he shoveled goodie (Yellow Pages) after competitive goodie (CPE sales) at the BOC's to help them survive.

Thrive is the more appropriate word. Most states, fearful that divestiture would mean disaster for their BOC's, granted generous rate increases. In the first two-and-a-half years following divestiture, local rates for residential service increased an average of 45 percent—an annual rate of increase of 16 percent (Pollack 1986). The BOC's, equally fearful of divestiture, implemented long-overdue cost-cutting measures. As a result, they posted return-on-equity figures in the range of 11 percent to 14 percent for 1984, the first postdivestiture year, and ROE's in the range of 14 percent to 15 percent (Hayes 1986) in 1985. Not bad for Grandma Bell. It should come as no surprise, though—after all, the BOC's do control the access line, the closest thing to a monopoly left in telecommunications.

But the regional holding companies, new parents to the BOC's, recognize that the monopoly is not forever and have undertaken aggressive diversification strategies. The regionals have spread into international markets, computer servicing, international directory sales, real-estate development, and retail computer stores. Each regional has a somewhat different portfolio from its siblings, but none has pulled together a coherent grand strategy for its competitive ventures.[6]

All over the map, the BOC's have embraced market competition as a way of life with varying enthusiasm. U.S. West has led the battle for more competition, less regulation, and removal of the MFJ restrictions on the BOC's. The firm has supported deregulation legislation in the states in which it operates and has had some partial successes, such as Oregon's legislation (*Telecommunications Reports* 1985b) and Nebraska's aggressively deregulatory 1986 legislation. U.S. West has committed publicly to open competition, but others still retain the regulatory habit. U.S. West and its hard-charger CEO, Jack MacAllister, were criticized by an executive at another regional (Maremont 1985): "This is not the time for uncontrolled, cowboy kind of competition." One executive is looking forward to the industry's competitive future, the other is looking back to the regulatory past.

The regional holding companies have also talked tough about how competitive they are, but talk is cheap when 95 percent of your revenues still come from local phone customers. Their mettle has yet to be tested against savvy competitors in a battle for a major market. If, for example, AT&T got serious about bypassing the BOC's to its big customers in the fifty largest downtown areas of the country, it is likely that many BOC's would run to the regulators and ask for protection, rather than run to their customers with better and cheaper service packages.

And what of AT&T, darling of the stock-market analysts in 1982, inheritor of the golden future of the information age? To those of us doing AT&T's financial analyses in the months just prior to divestiture, such predictions were taken as executive hype and market analysts' myopia. We saw a business portfolio consisting of:

A cash-hungry, overstaffed, and over-regulated AT&T-Communications, ill-equipped to fight off competitors;

A bloated marketing and sales organization, AT&T–Information Systems, unable to deliver on its financial commitments in the fiercely competitive CPE markets and draining nearly a billion dollars a year from the corporation; and

A manufacturing arm, Western Electric, that was about to lose its captive BOC customers and was floundering into ill-advised foreign ventures. With little hope of capturing new markets or effectively fending off competitors in its traditional markets, Western had nothing to gain and everything to lose.

As if the individual details weren't depressing enough, at the time of divestiture, the entire firm was poorly prepared to deal with the new environment. First, the FCC's *Second Computer Inquiry* rules mandated that AT&T-IS could only deal with AT&T-C on an arm's-length basis. Consequently, AT&T was effectively prohibited from being a systems vendor.

Second, marketing and sales (AT&T-IS) and its supplier (Western Electric) were separate organizations with conflicting objectives. An AT&T-IS executive, who had formerly worked at Digital Equipment Corp., stated during a 1983 conversation with me that "...the difference between AT&T-IS and DEC is that at DEC, the enemy was IBM; at AT&T-IS, the enemy is Western Electric."

Third, and perhaps most important, top management failed to adopt a coherent strategy for the new AT&T. With no clear view of what businesses AT&T would and would not be in, executives throughout the firm tried to carve out new activities, new products, and new services, usually in conflict with one another. Middle management's time was occupied with turf battles and other forms of internecine warfare, and top management seemed to be unable to make the tough decisions needed to sort out the business.

The picture at the end of 1983 was a bit too pessimistic, but only a bit. AT&T-Communications slimmed down its staff, used its existing capacity more efficiently so that capital expenditures were kept to a minimum, and learned to outmarket its rivals. For the first time in years, the long-distance business generated positive cash flow.[7]

AT&T-IS and Western Electric, beset by their own problems and locked in mortal combat, were poor market performers. In preparation for divestiture, both organizations believed that AT&T needed to be in the computer business, and that they should lead the effort. Western believed that it could sell its 3B line of processors—manufactured as the core of its switching and PBX systems for the BOC's—as stand-alone computers to the non-Bell market as a means to production-scale economies. Unfortunately, the world didn't need a clone of DEC's VAX, a successful circa-1975 minicomputer, which the 3B line most closely resembled. AT&T-IS believed that it could sell a high-powered IBM-compatible micro as a way of achieving economies of scope in its use of its sales force. As a result of this battle, each went its own way: AT&T-IS sold its Olivetti-manufactured micro while Western peddled its 3B series. Top management was unwilling or unable to set a single direction for AT&T's entry into the computer business, so it ended up with two contradictory and half-hearted efforts.

In 1985, AT&T rationalized the organization of its competitive side by doing away with Western Electric as a separate entity and integrating its manufacturing operations into the market-defined organizations they serve.

In 1986, following further relaxation of the structural-separation rules in the FCC's *Third Computer Inquiry*, AT&T announced a reorganization that will bring together its long-distance carrier, AT&T-Communications, with its equipment vendor, AT&T–Information Systems. When this change is completed, AT&T may at last be prepared to reach its full potential.

After the troubles of 1907, Theodore Vail set a clear strategic course for Bell that it followed for over half a century. Every employee knew what the Bell System stood for, and every customer knew what to expect from the Bell System. Today, the new AT&T does not yet have such a compelling mission. Neither recently retired Chairman Brown nor new CEO James Olsen appear to be able to set the firm on a new strategic course. Perhaps a corporation gets only one Theodore Vail in its history.

The Regulatory Game, Once Again

Although Chairman Brown had hoped that the divestiture had put an end "...to the arduous experience of debating, testing, exploring, proposing and counter-proposing that has been going on continuously for so many years..." (Brown 1982), it was just getting underway in earnest.

Federal Communications Commission

In the years since divestiture, the FCC has pursued a number of economically based policy objectives:

Regulate carrier and subscriber access charges imposed by the BOC's;

Gradually reduce the subsidy burden on long-distance to support subscriber access costs and recover those costs by the direct levy of a monthly subscriber line charge to each subscriber;

Move the BOC's and AT&T-Communications toward "cost-based pricing";

Impose the *Second Computer Inquiry* structural-separation rules on the BOC's, but gradually remove them from AT&T in accord with the findings of the *Third Computer Inquiry;* and

Advocate lifting the MFJ restriction against the entry of BOC's into the long-distance market.

For the BOC's, filing access charge tariffs was their first direct contact with the FCC, a regulatory body that AT&T had always dealt with for them. BOC access charges were squarely in the FCC's jurisdiction, however, and the FCC had a plan. A very large part of the BOC costs to be covered by carrier access charges were the costs of customers' access lines (local loops) and other costs that did not vary with usage (non-traffic-sensitive, or NTS, costs), which represented the subsidy from toll to local. The FCC's long-term plan was gradually to phase out the recovery of these costs from the carriers through their usage rates and to recover them instead from a monthly subscriber line charge on each customer.

The plan almost became derailed when the FCC announced its intention to phase in subscriber line charges in April of 1984. Although the FCC proposed a modest $2.00 charge for residence lines (higher for business lines) to start with, their eventual target was $7.00 per line. In the wake of divestiture and the concerns that local rates would increase, Congress took this as evidence that its worst nightmares were all true. The FCC was called on the carpet in early 1984 and told quite emphatically by Congress that now was not the time for subscriber line charges. Judge Greene, who had a clear idea of how he wanted access charges levied, fulminated from the bench about the FCC's plan. The FCC could afford to ignore Greene, but not Congress.

The FCC learned its political lessons well from this fiasco; the access charge plan went ahead, but not on schedule. In addition, the FCC made sure that after the first relatively modest subscriber line charge went into effect, AT&T filed for a substantial decrease in long-distance rates. The joint timing emphasized the *quid pro quo* nature of the FCC's plan.

Carrier access charges also played an important role as the BOC's completed the conversion of their switches to provide equal access to all long-distance carriers. The competitive carriers had complained for years that their access was far inferior to AT&T's, which justified the 55 percent (and more) discount that the ENFIA tariff gave them. However, achieving equal access to the BOC switches had a corollary: The competitive carriers sooner or later would have to pay the same access charges as AT&T.

Now that the competitive carriers were getting what they said they wanted in 1979, were they happy?

> William English, Senior Vice President, Satellite Business Systems: "There is a very real danger the industry will not be viable. It's all in jeopardy, the whole historic experiment of trying to bring competition to long-distance communications."
>
> William McGowan, Chairman, MCI Corporation: "The process is so biased in AT&T's favor that for most customers, equal access equals AT&T."
>
> James Blaszak, attorney for a competitive-carrier customer-lobbying group: "We're all for deregulation, but until there is effective competition, we don't want to be without regulatory protection."

All quotes are from Maremont and Wilke (1985). Apparently, the ENFIA discount had been worth much more to them than equal access, and the market was exposing the facts that years of regulatory muddle had failed to uncover: without the deep discount, the competitive carriers were not so competitive. Their earnings performance confirmed this.

The FCC, to its great credit, resisted the enormous political pressure to maintain the AT&T price umbrella for the competitive carriers. In February 1985, Representative John W. Bryant (D-Tex) introduced a bill in Congress that would require local phone companies to continue charging the new carriers less than AT&T in each market. The FCC opposed the bill and continued to press its policy of equal access, equal access charges.

Since divestiture was the ultimate structural prescription to separate monopoly and competitive services, the role of the *Second Computer Inquiry* rules, the FCC's previous structural solution, needed clarifying. The BOC's had been permitted to operate a variety of competitive businesses by the modified MFJ, so they were obviously in need of structural separation. However, the case for other structural safeguards was not at all clear, and the FCC acted to remove them, first by accommodating an AT&T reorganization in 1985 to consolidate AT&T-IS and then, in 1986, by accommodating the reintegration of AT&T-C and AT&T-IS.

The reasoning behind this rule relaxation was simple and compelling: There was no market power to protect against, and the very considerable costs of separation were hurting both AT&T and its customers. The Justice Department claimed that "the costs of maintaining separation for the provision of CPE now outweigh the benefits," and customers also supported lifting the restrictions. A large number of equipment manufacturers and their lobbying groups claimed that "AT&T could compete unfairly in the unregulated CPE and information processing markets; and effective regulatory safeguards must be retained to protect ratepayers and AT&T competitors" (*Telecommunications Reports* 1985a). Most vehement were six of the seven regional holding companies, who were adamantly against lifting restrictions from AT&T unless restrictions were also lifted from them. Despite this opposition, the FCC eventually removed the unnecessary and costly restrictions on AT&T, two years after divestiture.

Slowly and inexorably, the FCC was pushing the enormously cumbersome regulatory process in a direction that would correct the most egregious inefficiencies of the past. With a constancy of purpose unusual in regulatory history, the commission slogged through the self-serving pleadings for special protections and eventually reached sensible decisions. Of course, it took years to accomplish changes that a competitive market would have achieved in days, but this is the very best we can expect from the regulatory process: agonizingly slow progress in the right direction.

In one instance, however, the FCC continued an egregious regulatory inefficiency: "cost-based pricing." Since the mid-1970s, the commission had favored accounting methods for assigning and allocating historical costs, including overheads and common costs, to individual services, and then used those costs on which to base rates. Virtually the entire body of normative analysis in regulatory economics condemns this practice: Historical allocated costs bear no relation to forward-looking incremental economic costs. Firms in competitive industries must relate their prices to their economic costs, and successful ones have little trouble doing so in practice. However, measuring such costs in ways that stand up to hostile cross-examination in an adjudicatory proceeding is effectively impossible. It is much safer to provide the wrong costs precisely — since the accounting numbers will stand up in court — than the right costs imprecisely. As virtually all regulatory commissions before them, the FCC has chosen the former course.[8] About the only thing in favor of using wrong but precise cost numbers is that it removes one more reason for interminable discussion, proposal, and counterproposal, of which both state and federal regulators have had plenty since divestiture.

The FCC's argument not to restrict the BOC's from entry into the long-distance market was made to Judge Greene in an *amicus curiae* brief (FCC 1982). Simply, the FCC believed the BOC's could offer real competition to AT&T and thought it worth the minimal risk (now that equal access had been specified and mandated). Clearly, the judge and Justice disagreed.

The District Court and the Department of Justice

The new regulator in town, Judge Greene, continued to award and withhold the spoils. The regional holding companies would apply for line-of-business waivers, which were then reviewed by the Justice Department for conformity with the intent of the settlement. After hearing Justice's recommendations, Judge Greene would decide if he agreed. Out of eighty-six BOC-requested waivers, the new regulator granted fifty-three (see Chapter 5).

By mid-1986, the entire industry had grown tired of regulatory amateurs. Senator Robert Dole (R-Kan) introduced a bill in Congress to incorporate the provisions of the MFJ into the FCC's rules and to move oversight of the decree from Judge Greene to the FCC (*Telecommunications Reports* 1986a). No doubt Dole thought he was merely clearing up some procedural details left over from divestiture.

To Dole's great surprise, the lobbyists struck like sharks in a feeding frenzy. Quickest to the kill was the American Newspaper

Publishers Association, an extraordinarily effective lobbying group skilled at posing defenses of their own economic interests as "protecting the First Amendment."[9] ANPA had successfully lobbied a media-conscious Judge Greene to insist that the MFJ contain a provision to forestall AT&T's entry into electronic publishing (such as videotext). ANPA was not about to lose a competitive advantage for its members, and it immediately and loudly opposed the Dole bill. In a statement that will stand forever as a monument to self-serving double-talk, ANPA Executive Vice President Jerry W. Freidheim said, "Unless the bill is introduced with adequate safeguards to protect and promote electronic publishing competition, ANPA will have to oppose the bill as anticompetitive." (*Telecommunications Reports* 1986b). This, from a representative of the only nonregulated U.S. industry to have successfully lobbied Congress for a law granting it permanent antitrust immunity (save the limited immunity of some professional sports).

Judge Greene took a dim view of transferring oversight of the decree to the FCC, stating his suspicions not only of the regional holding companies but of the FCC:

...If the regional companies are left completely to their own devices... with their vast financial power [they] could crush their smaller competitors which do not have a huge rate base from which to finance advertising campaigns, price manipulations, marketing infrastructures, service policies, and the like.

On the FCC, Judge Greene opined that "the philosophy of the FCC is...to relate price to cost, irrespective of other considerations." (*Telecommunications Reports* 1986a). What anticompetitive evil lurks in relating price to cost or a firm's having a service policy or a "marketing infrastructure" (whatever that may be), the jurist declines to say.

State Regulators

Having been awakened from their multidecade doze by the AT&T–Justice settlement, state regulators reacted to divestiture in near-total panic. Canny BOC's capitalized on the regulators' fears and filed for healthy rate increases for their basic services. State regulators did very well by their BOC's, putting them in the best financial positions they had seen in years.

Though competition was the watchword in Washington, it certainly did not play in Sacramento or other state capitals. According to Administrative Law Judge Patrick Power of the California Public Utilities Commission (1984): "In the stormy turbulent circumstances of divestiture, there is one beacon that guides us—universal service...." To state regulators, universal service meant keeping basic exchange rates low, which meant continued subsidies from long-distance to the exchange companies via access charges. At the same time, however, competitive long-distance meant lower costs to the voters, so that looked good as well.

State regulators faced two critical decisions postdivestiture: setting access charges for intrastate, inter-LATA long-distance, and opening the intrastate long-distance market, either inter-LATA or intra-LATA, to competition. It is a measure of the confusion among the state commissions that the resolution of these two issues varies considerably from state to state.

> Several southern states, California, and Oregon have set their access charges above 9.5¢ per minute, while Illinois, New Jersey, and others have set them at less than 7¢ per minute. The spread between the lowest (New Jersey) and the highest (Alabama) is 7¢ (Noll 1986).
>
> California has proposed that long-distance carriers must block all intra-LATA calls, while Indiana would like the carriers to pay Indiana Bell for all such calls they carry. A number of states have permitted intra-LATA competition simply because they saw no effective way to prohibit it (Noll 1986).

A number of state commissions have actually been aggressively deregulating certain telephone services such as Centrex, a PBX-like service offered from the BOC central office, and inside wiring on the customer's premises, connecting the phone to the outside wires (*MIS Week* 1985). In Oregon, new legislation permits the commissioner to deregulate virtually any service if competition exists. Nebraska has passed legislation that precludes their regulatory commission from acting on any rate change of any telephone company unless that rate increase is above 10 percent or 2 percent of consumers petition the commission for review. Illinois has passed deregulatory legislation, and the Vermont commission has proposed far-reaching legislation to abolish regulation altogether in return for a prescribed cap on increases in the basic subscription rate.

Arkansas, on the other hand, issued an order preserving the Southwestern Bell monopoly on intra-LATA long-distance. Flexible tariffs have been permitted in New York and certain other states.

The Regulatory Process

What has not changed is the regulatory process. In all jurisdictions, competitors still seek advantage through litigation and regulation, not in the marketplace. Regulators often still view their job as balancing equities rather than achieving efficiencies. Even the FCC, with clear efficiency objectives and the will to pursue them, finds that due process and interminable hearings are its primary product, not the improvement of industry performance. State regulators, far more confused and far less informed, see their job as dividing the spoils and achieving distributive equity. Charles Stalon of the Illinois Commerce Commission stated it right out: "The first responsibility of a state public utility commission (PUC) is not to facilitate the efficient workings of the economic system, but to use the power of government to protect certain interest groups *from* the efficient workings of the system" (Stalon 1984).

Today's survivors in telecommunications have learned that playing the regulatory game is far more important than pleasing the customer.

MCI, blooded in its early regulatory battles with AT&T, has built its success on its hard-earned regulatory prowess. Long known within the industry as a "law firm with an antenna on the roof" (Wilke and Maremont 1986), MCI found that over 80 percent of its costs to set up its first microwave route were regulatory and legal, not construction and operations. Until recently, MCI's two most valuable assets were its right to discounted access (the 55-percent ENFIA discount) and its $1.8 billion antitrust award, pending from AT&T. MCI's stock price has been most responsive to the health of these two assets, much more than to the firm's ability to transport long-distance phone calls. When the antitrust damage award was cut to $37.8 million on appeal, the price of MCI stock took a nosedive, reflecting the relative importance of regulatory and legal matters over telecommunications matters for the firm.

Southwestern Bell has responded to the competitive challenge of shared tenant services (STS), not in the marketplace, but through the regulatory process. At the behest of Southwestern, Kansas has placed an outright ban on STS, and Arkansas is adopting an effective STS ban as well (*MIS Week* 1985).

AT&T continues to give strong support to the MFJ ban on entry of the BOC's into the long-distance market. While both the BOC's and the FCC have argued that such entry would provide a needed competitive spur to AT&T, AT&T has used the Justice Department and Judge Greene to protect their home long-distance market from these most serious potential competitors.

As long as there are regulators, there will be handicapping, there will be firms seeking to disadvantage competitors. There will be newspaper publishers seeking to foreclose entry of AT&T into a new and exciting field (videotext) that AT&T might have brought to consumers first, if it had had the chance. Will consumers know what they missed? Not likely. There will be equipment manufacturers who will be anxious to saddle AT&T and the BOC's with extra restrictions in CPE markets. Will consumers know what products were not available to them as a result of such restrictions? Not likely. There will always be BOC's trying to keep long-distance carriers out of the local exchange market. Will consumers ever know what new technologies could have delivered cheaper and better local access with competition? Not likely. There will always be long-distance carriers who want to keep the BOC's out of long-distance. Will consumers ever know how much lower prices could have been if the BOC's had been permitted to be aggressive long-distance competitors? Not likely.[9]

Notes

1. This restriction was later lifted.
2. Those who failed to choose were assigned carriers in proportion to the outcome in that region.
3. Conversion of independent company exchanges to equal access will take considerably longer, especially in the case of small rural telephone companies who plead that such conversion is too costly.
4. A typical operation is OlympiaNet, a joint venture between Olympia & York, a commercial real-estate venture, and United Telecommunications, an independent phone company; see Flax (1984).
5. The FCC's *Second Computer Inquiry* rules state that the BOC's can only sell CPE through a fully separated subsidiary. In each of the seven regions, this subsidiary is located with the regional holding company.

6. Southwestern Bell seems to be the exception. The firm has concentrated its competitive activities exclusively on the low-tech but high-profit Yellow Pages business, aggressively expanding its directory operations into forty-eight states and overseas.
7. Long-distance had always generated substantial earnings, but had required huge cash outlays for new equipment. Cash outflow (operating expenses plus new capital expenditures) had usually exceeded cash inflow (revenues).
8. An exception is the Interstate Commerce Commission, which has adopted a stand-alone cost ceiling on rail freight prices.
9. For a similar critique of regulation *cum* competition, see Kahn (1984).

References

Brown, C.L. 1982. "Statement" Press release upon announcement of the divestiture decision, January 8.

FCC. *Amicus Curiae* Brief to District Court, pp. 29–52 (1982).

Flax, S. 1984. "The Latest Way to Foil the Phone Monopoly." *Fortune* (April 2): 108–111.

Hayes, J. 1986. "Telecommunications." *Forbes* (see also *Forbes* January 14, 1985, pp. 208–209) (January 13): 210–211.

Kahn, A.E. 1984. "The Uneasy Marriage of Regulation and Competition." *Telematics* (September 5): 1–17.

Maremont, M. 1985. "The Baby Bells Take Giant Steps." *Business Week* (September 2): 94–104.

———. 1986. "AT&T: The Giant Hasn't Made Many False Moves." *Business Week* (February 17): 88–89.

Maremont, M., and J. Wilke. 1985. "Is the Long-Distance Deck Stacked in AT&T's Favor?" *Business Week* (February 25): 101–102.

Mason, T., and M. Maremont. 1985. "Selling Switching Systems: The Jostling Gets Rough." *Business Week* (June 3): 82–83.

MIS Week. 1985. "State Deregulation." Special series, July 17, August 14, August 21, September 4, September 11, October 9, October 16.

Noll, R. 1986. "State Regulatory Responses to Competition and Divestiture in the Telecommunications Industry." In *Antitrust and Regulation*, edited by R.E. Grieson. Lexington, Mass.: Lexington Books.

Pollack, A. 1986. "Phone Rate Increases Found Below Dire Predictions of '84." *New York Times*, June 16, p. 2.

Power, P. *Proposed Decision 83-06-91.* State of California Public Utilities Commission, pp. 190–191 (1984).

Rudolph, B. 1986. "Ratifying a Winner in the Phone Vote." *Time* (August 25): 44.

Stalon, C. 1984. "Comments." In *Telecommunications Access and Public Policy*, edited by M.A. Baughcum and G.R. Faulhaber, p. 232, Norwood, N.J.: Ablex Publishing.

Telecommunications Reports. 1985a. April 15, p. 40.

———. 1985b. June 17, pp. 1–2.

———. 1986a. June 9, pp. 1–3.

———. 1986b. June 16, p. 2.

Wenders, J.T. 1986. *The Economics of Telecommunications.* Cambridge, Mass.: Ballinger Publishing Co.

Wilke, J. 1985. "The Small Fry in Phones Are Getting Cut Off" *Business Week* (November 4): 98.

Wilke, J., and M. Maremont. 1986. "The Long-Distance Warrior." *Business Week* (February 17): 90.

CHAPTER 8

The Future of Telecommunications: An Immodest Proposal

The sweet smell of profit has attracted many firms to the new telecommunications game. The inventive genius unlocked by the digital-electronics revolution has supplied, and will continue to supply, the products on which these firms pin their hopes for commercial success. And yet the quite-visible hand of the regulator is even more pervasive, even more deadening today than before divestiture. The regulatory game continues to dominate both the engineers and the marketeers. The complex and subtle interplay among technology, markets, and politics continues. While politics has lost the power to control, it has not lost the power to destroy.

Industry Prospects

Under the current regulatory regime of high technology and low politics, where is this industry heading? Forecasting the future of telecommunications has become a growth industry in recent years, with predictable results—the only accurate forecast was that all the forecasts would be way off the mark. However, a careful examination of the underlying technological, economic, and political facts does permit some tentative conclusions.

The Long-Distance Market

The recent success of AT&T-Communications suggests that they have learned to translate their awesome technical and operational prowess into serious marketing clout. It is doubtful that the small fry, such as MCI and Sprint, will be able to drive AT&T much below a 70-percent share of the market, unless they are able to revamp their current strategies.

There will continue to be strong pressures to exclude the BOC's from the long-distance market. AT&T will play as many chips as it needs in the regulatory game, both at the FCC and with Judge Greene and the Justice Department, to keep the BOC's inside their LATAs. They will be ably assisted in this effort by the competitive carriers, whose position would become even more precarious should the BOC's be allowed into long-distance.

IBM will continue desultory attempts to crack this market through third parties, as in their aborted SBS effort and their cautious partnership with MCI. They will not, however, risk regulatory capture of their computer profits by full-scale entry into a still-regulated business.

Unless Congress or a new administration changes its mandate, the FCC will likely continue its thrust to eliminate the subsidy from toll to the access line, shifting access charges away from carriers and toll usage and onto customers via the subscriber line charge. Although they may permit AT&T some pricing flexibility for certain services, full deregulation of AT&T is unlikely, for several reasons. First, the FCC will wish to retain the ability to force AT&T to cut long-distance rates as subscriber-line charges increase, in order to demonstrate that such increases do have offsetting benefits. Second, AT&T's very success in maintaining a high market share will be taken as evidence of continued market power, hence a continued need for regulatory control. Third, the FCC will face continued demands by rural customers for the same rates that are enjoyed by customers less costly to serve. To meet those demands, the FCC must continue its regulation to prohibit AT&T from rate deaveraging or abandoning service.

Today and for the foreseeable future, fiber optics is the technology of choice for long-distance transmission. Virtually all carriers are committed to expansion with fiber-optic systems of very great capacity. The present industry situation is lots and lots of very cheap intercity transmission capacity. On the switching front, comlete digitalization of the network looks to be probable. A "smart" long-distance network would enable large users to reconfigure their corporate private line and WATS networks on a daily or even hourly basis.

The long-distance market seems to be evolving into a classic service market, like retailing. Although there would appear to be no great trick to conducting a retail-store operation, Sears Roebuck and Bloomingdale's somehow consistently outperform their competitors in their individual markets, with correspondingly superior financial results. Similarly, the technology of long-distance is well understood and the required capital investment has not presented a barrier to entry to competitors. However, some firms seem to understand better than others how to give customers what they want more cost-effectively than the next guy. Today, that firm is AT&T. Their recent success in the market has shown that customers want more than plain long-distance; they want operator services, immediate credit on misdialed calls, and the reliability that MCI and others can't yet deliver. In such markets, good service will beat low price every time, and until other vendors who can provide that service enter the long-distance market, AT&T should continue to rule the roost.

The lack of strong competitive pressures in this market may permit continued inefficiencies, rate averaging, for one. AT&T may try to break out of this regulatory box, but may be powerless against rural lobbies (independent rural telephone companies, legislators from rural states) that wish to maintain their subsidy.

Another problem is that AT&T only needs to reduce its bloated costs minimally to beat the less-than-effective competitors it currently faces. Had the MFJ permitted the BOC's, the only other varsity-class players in the game, to enter this market, substantially more competitive pressure would be exerted to reduce operating costs.

Regulatory "cost-based pricing" will be a source of trouble, difficult to detect. Its most likely victims will be any new services that AT&T might offer, which the FCC is likely to saddle with accounting costs of allocated overheads, in the name of preventing cross-subsidy. Many new services would never survive infancy with prices reflecting such uneconomic costs, and so would never be delivered at all.

Although it is the lack of competitive pressure in the long-distance market that permits these inefficiencies, it would be a mistake to take this lack as an excuse to re-regulate long-distance. Indeed, it appears that it is the continued presence of regulation, either by the FCC or Judge Greene, that is responsible for the failure of able companies to take on AT&T in this market.

Access and Local Service

The opportunities for access and local service are as great as the uncertainties that cloud the future of these markets. What are these market opportunities?

Shared tenant service (STS) may be the most important market opportunity in the medium term. The BOC's can be active participants in this market, but its ultimate profitability is still in doubt.

"Bypass" is likely to be a transient phenomenon. The FCC has shown its determination to discontinue the subsidy from toll to local access, so it is unlikely that firms will be willing to make big investments in bypass to avoid a "tax" that probably won't be around in five years. In some markets, though, economic efficiency rather than "tax" avoidance may prompt a large firm or an STS operator to institute direct access to interexchange carriers.

Cellular radio could develop into the alternative technology of choice within the next decade. Currently, cellular radio is the basis of the new mobile-phone service, aimed at an upscale, urban market. Further advances may mean that radiotelephony will eventually be able to serve economically the mass market for access—stationary phones in subscribers' homes—thus providing a true competitive alternative to the local access monopoly. In some submarkets, such as rural subscribers, cellular may now be a viable access alternative to the miles of expensive copper-wire access lines now strung to farms across the country.

These competitive services constitute both opportunities and threats to the BOC's. They suggest new ways to approach traditional BOC markets, new ways to apply technology, and new ways to make money for the BOC's. At the same time, they are attractive to potential competitors, including AT&T and other BOC's, who can invade the traditional markets of the BOC's, stealing "their" customers and "their" revenues. And therein lies the source of the uncertainties hovering over these markets: how will the BOC's respond to entry into their markets?

Should the BOC's opt for an aggressively procompetitive strategy, they are likely to be restrained by state regulators as well as by Judge Greene and the Justice Department. As the custodians of the bottleneck access line, the BOC's will be severely limited in their ability to offer new or enhanced services because of regulatory fears of cross-subsidy and denial of access. Competitors will claim anticompetitive conduct and demand regulatory protection from the BOC's. Consumer advocates will claim that their money is being used to finance competitive ventures and that basic access is being neglected.

Should the BOC's opt for a conservative public-utility strategy, they will attempt to convince their state regulators that competition will mean less revenues with which to achieve universal service. Further, they will point out that each time an STS or a bypass competitor encroaches on BOC territory, any previous BOC investment in that business will be "stranded" (unused) and must be recovered from other ratepayers.

This public utility strategy attempts to build a regulatory wall around the business that denies entry to all—the Bell System's strategy for many years. In the short run, a responsive regulator can make this procedure wildly successful. However, as the Bell System found, the exercise of this strategy sows the seeds of its own destruction. When the regulator is forced to respond to customers who want to know why they cannot have the same advanced products and services available to their branch offices in other states, when the regulator is forced to turn away dozens of competitors with a demonstrated ability to please consumers, all in the name of protecting BOC revenues, that regulator will soon begin to wonder whose game it is playing.

Unfortunately, the competitive strategy is equally perilous, because it may be competitive in name only. Other players will claim that their access to customers has been denied, or at least crimped, by the BOC's. Regulatory handicapping will be called for, and the BOC's will spend more time on regulatory proceedings than on actual competition. In these proceedings, the word "competition" will be used quite often, and admiringly, but most activities will probably be directed at protecting one or another party *from* competition, which is, after all, what regulation is about. This should sound familiar; it describes the point/counterpoint of Bell System strategy and regulatory response during the late 1970s and early 1980s.

What are the likely outcomes of these two strategies? Playing public utility is likely to produce significant short-term gains followed by much pain and suffering. Playing competitive is likely to involve lots of short-term frustration with a moderate chance of long-term success. Predictably, the BOC's have exhibited a good deal of variation in their strategic choices. U.S. West, for example, is playing the aggressive competitor role, with rather more *brio* as well as more success than Charles Brown did with the old Bell System. Southwestern Bell, on the other hand, is playing "public utility" fairly consistently, stamping out competition with the help of their regulators (*MIS Week* 1985a).

Antitrust, Yet Again

There is, however, a hazard in the public utility strategy that threatens not only the BOC's that follow it but the entire industry— the likelihood of significant private antitrust suits against BOC attempts to maintain their regulated monopoly. During the debates of the 1970s, the old Bell System consistently tried to block entry through regulation and by denying access, justifying its actions to regulators and the public in the name of universal service. Not only did that justification do nothing to forestall the government and private antitrust suits, it sounded awfully weak to the juries. Similarly, today's efforts to stop competition from bypass or STS operators are justified in the name of low subscriber rates. However, when a frustrated competitor brings a private antitrust suit against a BOC, anticompetitive behavior, whatever the regulatory justification, simply will not wash.

Customer Premises Equipment

This market provides us with a model for competitive telecommunications. Many firms offer a wide variety of equipment and services, and no firm threatens to dominate the market. Nevertheless, attempts to lessen regulation of the BOC's to make them more effective competitors in the CPE market have been vigorously opposed by industry lobbyists for CPE vendors, as was the case in Colorado (*MIS Week* 1985b).

The comparative freedom from regulatory constraint in this market has induced its own curious inefficiencies. As custodians of the bottleneck access line, the BOC's have not been permitted to offer certain enhanced services that could most economically be provided from the central office switch. For example, customers that use the network to transmit data among computers that have differing data codes and protocols (for example, which bit streams signal "stand by to receive data" or "end of message") find that they must develop or purchase systems that convert those codes and protocols before their computers can talk to one another. Obviously, this function would be much more efficiently performed through a single code-and-protocol conversion system at each telephone central switch rather than through systems at all customer locations. However, code-and-protocol conversion has been classified as an enhanced service that can only be offered by a BOC under *Second Computer Inquiry* rules, that is, through a separate subsidiary with no common equipment. Such rules eliminate any efficiencies that the BOC could bring to the task through the sharing of common equipment. As a consequence, this important function is still being provided via the customer's own equipment.

Code-and-protocol conversion is but a single example of how intelligence can be used, or misused, in the telecommunications network. In some cases, intelligence, or enhanced service, is most efficiently located in the CPE; in other cases, the local switch is the obvious economic choice; in yet others, the toll switch is the optimal location. Regulatory concerns about mixing competitive enhanced services with bottleneck facilities have resulted in rules that are actively driving the intelligence function out of the network and into CPE. The result: a higher-cost system. Of course, the competitive CPE market will supply what's demanded, but the demands will be shaped by the regulatory rules prohibiting or inhibiting an efficient supply of intelligence functions in the network. Further, now that CPE manufacturers are tooled up to supply high-function PBX and key systems, any change in the rules about network-supplied intelligence, under active consideration by the FCC in its *Third Computer Inquiry*, has been and will continue to be vigorously resisted by the lobbyists of these manufacturers.

Service Provider Equipment

The market for large-scale switching and transmission systems for operating-company use has many global players, each capable of providing state-of-the-art products and high-quality service. The threat to the competitiveness of this market comes not from traditional regulation but from trade protectionism. Many of the competitors in the U.S. market are Japanese, European, or Canadian. Should the share of U.S. firms in this market shrink to less than 50 percent, we can expect the usual accusations of dumping, unfair competition, "coolie labor," and so forth that generally precede demands for higher import tariffs. The bottom line for consumers: higher rates for service.

Industry Prospects: Conclusion

The industry will probably continue to suffer from economic inefficiencies caused by the regulatory process, although the engine of technology, the incurable optimism of entrepreneurs, and the necessary responses of the larger players will keep the industry moving forward. New products and services will be introduced, and costs will decline, but regulation will both retard and distort these trends. The good news is that the industry will undergo irrepressible growth; the bad news it that the special interests, playing the regulatory game, will do their level best to repress and distort that growth to their advantage.

A risk perceived by many is that large customers, firms and other institutions, will have the economic wherewithal to avoid regulation and deploy sophisticated technology to bypass the local distribution system, while less advantaged users will have to put up with retarded innovation, higher costs, and continued subsidies because they have no alternative to regulatory control. What could develop is a two-tier telecommunications system, with those who can escape the dead hand of regulation moving toward a high-tech, efficient competitive system divorced from an increasingly obsolete, regulated public system.

Perhaps the most serious long-term challenge the industry faces in its present configuration is that a significant number of BOC's will attempt to play the regulated-monopoly/universal-service game with their regulators. Should this be their strategy of choice, these BOC's will have effectively duplicated all the problems of the old Bell System: monopoly and competitive services offered by one firm; control of the bottleneck facility; use of the regulatory process to enforce anticompetitive measures, such as prohibiting STS and intra-LATA long-distance entry. We have been down this road before, and we know where it ends: antitrust court. The last thing the American people need for their telephone system is another round of inept policy solutions dictated from the bench.

Regulation Is the Problem, Not the Solution

In more innocent days, economists and other policy analysts saw the economic system as rife with the disease of market failure and prescribed government regulation as the cure. Our present, more cynical view is that regulation is a far more virulent disease, for which the cure is more competition. Abbott Lipsky (1986) expresses the prevailing opinion:

The original regulatory schemes were based on unduly pessimistic views of competition and unduly optimistic views of regulation.... It was also recognized that regulatory agencies suffer from inherent institutional flaws that prevent recognition or prompt reform of their mistakes. It seems that agencies adopt as their first priority their own growth and survival. They tend to reach out for new jurisdiction and to extend their control as widely as possible. Given the opportunity, administrative agencies seek to create benefits that can be transferred, in one form or another, to the Congressional and executive-branch decision-makers on whom they depend for their budgets and their statutory authority. By far the most effective means for producing such benefits is to restrict competition within the regulated industry, or between the regulated industry and its actual or potential competitors. Agencies that have these powers exploit them aggressively; those that do not have such powers actively seek them.

Little wonder that the historical evidence on regulatory performance is so negative. Little wonder that the specific history of telecommunications regulation, reviewed in Chapter 3, reveals a dismal record of dealing with the market failures of this industry. Little wonder that virtually every problem anticipated for the future of telecommunications has its origins in regulation.

A True Regulatory Parable

The problems of regulation are not limited either to telecommunications or to the United States. Some insight into how regulation really works can be gained from considering United Parcel Service's efforts to extend its package-delivery service to the Canadian province of Ontario.

Ontario had a number of enterprises providing package delivery, including the Post Office, Canadian Pacific (CP), and a number of smaller firms. The market for parcel delivery was not directly regulated. United Parcel Service (UPS), a U.S.-based firm with many years of experience both in the U.S. and Canada in retail delivery service, sought to enter this provincial market.

While parcel delivery was not regulated, truck licensing was; the Ontario Highway Transport Board had authority from the federal government to regulate interprovincial trucking, including the granting to trucking firms of licenses to operate. Since parcel delivery requires the use of trucks, UPS applied to the board for trucking licenses.

The private parcel carriers objected vigorously. As licensees of the board, they argued that further entry into the parcel business was unnecessary, since adequate service was already being provided by the existing carriers. UPS's entry would only decrease the revenues of the incumbent firms, such as CP. Since the board did not wish to harm its licensees in return for the speculative benefits UPS might bring, they denied UPS its license.

In fact, the board's opinion was actually written by CP's counsel. When this came to light, the board was forced to reconsider the case but expressed amazement that anyone could find this action offensive.

Meanwhile, pending the outcome of the board's deliberations, UPS actually did enter the parcel-delivery market, but without trucks. Instead, they used station wagons with trailers. Since they didn't need a special license to operate automobiles, they had "invented around" the regulations by using an inefficient substitute for a truck, but a substitute that was not, by regulatory definition, a truck.

This parable of the absurd illustrates three characteristics of regulation:

1. The inclination of regulators to involve themselves in activities far outside their intended jurisdiction. In Canada, a board regulating highway transport was also regulating parcel delivery; in U.S. telecommunications, an antitrust court is regulating the local telephone companies.
2. The willingness of regulators to preserve the revenues of incumbent firms by restricting entry of new firms, thus denying consumers the benefits of increased competition. In Canada, the board so favored the existing carriers that it let one of them write the decision; in U.S. telecommunications, many state commissions have prohibited intra-LATA

competition or restricted STS entry to protect the revenue stream of the local BOC's.
3. The ability of firms to "invent around" regulations, thereby gaining entry but incurring higher than necessary costs. In Canada, UPS used unlicensed station wagons with trailers rather than the more efficient trucks for which it had been denied a license; in U.S. telecommunications, processing and intelligence functions are built into CPE, even though this could be done more efficiently in the network, because of regulatory safeguards and restrictions.[1]

It may appear that this story must be an outer extreme, a particularly outrageous, certainly not typical example of regulatory excess. It is not. It is the way things are.

If It's So Bad, How Come It Doesn't Hurt?

The ability of regulators to do real damage is substantial but not unlimited. The last thing a regulatory commission needs is irate peasants advancing on the castle with pitchforks at the ready, so commissions tend to observe several rules, one of the most important being to avoid imposing harms that can be directly traced by the victims to regulation. Another useful gimmick is to describe inefficiencies as "victories," "protecting competition," or "helping poor people."

"Do No Direct Harm"

It is the nature of regulation that its most egregious inefficiencies tend to be invisible to the casual observer. Regulators avoid actions where the *direct* consequences are hurtful to an aware group of individuals. Thus, regulators will do almost anything to avoid the bankruptcy of a client firm (as the CAB's prederegulation experience showed) or an increase in telephone-subscriber rates. However, regulators are quite willing to impose *indirect* damage of incalculable measure. Thus, a firm with a new technology (or simply a lower price) can be denied entry quite easily, because the cost of that entry to incumbent firms who would lose business is direct and obvious, but the benefits to consumers in the form of lower prices or better service are indirect and invisible. Those benefits are greater in magnitude than any losses to incumbent firms, but they are potential, hence invisible—consumers will never miss what they never had.[2]

Charles Schulze (1977: 23) emphasized this aspect of the American political economy:

Over the years the American political system has developed a set of formal and informal rules about losses associated with political decisions. First, we tend to subject political decisions to the rule, "Do no direct harm." We can let harms occur as the second- and third-order consequences of political action or through sheer inaction, but we cannot be seen to cause harm to anyone as the direct consequences of collective actions.

Doublespeak

The rhetoric of the regulatory process contributes to the confusion of who's doing what to whom: the most outrageously anticompetitive actions are justified as procompetitive, as when Judge Greene excluded AT&T from electronic publishing at the behest of ANPA, and the Colorado legislature killed the detariffing of Mountain Bell's CPE at the behest of North American Telecommunications Association, a group of interconnect manufacturers. Subsidies to rural areas and to the middle class, such as below-cost prices for access and rural long-distance, are justified as "helping poor people."

The system of "taxing" long-distance usage to subsidize below-cost prices for access is often characterized as taxing the rich (who are alleged to be heavy toll users) to subsidize the poor (who are alleged not to use toll). The evidence (Murphy 1981) is that household income only accounts for 2 to 10 percent of the variation in toll and local usage. Other demographic factors, such as size of household, age of head of household, and location (urban versus rural), are much more important in understanding who uses toll and who doesn't. Further, this is common knowledge among analysts who have actually studied the problem. Despite the facts, however, state regulators and others continue to defend the access subsidy as "helping the poor."

Asking the Fox to Guard the Henhouse

Economists have been leading critics of regulation, and many would find our analysis congenial to their professional views. It is a measure of the strength of the prevailing competitive climate that lawyers, policy analysts, and even many regulators agree that it is time to "unregulate," in the words of Mark Fowler, an FCC chairman.

Most observers and participants would also add that immediate deregulation of telecommunications is not politically feasible and we should expect a transition period, during which the industry would be guided toward full competition.

And who is to oversee this transition and guide the industry toward full competition? Why, the regulators, of course! The same regulators (and court) that could not solve the market failure problem or the problem of a single firm operating in both monopoly and competitive markets and that failed to execute properly Justice's divestiture plan are to oversee their own demise. As Lipsky (1986) suggests, deregulation is the last thing that most regulators want. The rhetoric about competition and "unregulation" is just that—rhetoric. We have sent the fox to guard the henhouse, and we should not be surprised at the result.

Even the regulatory commission with the strongest commitment to competition, the FCC, seems to have difficulty "unregulating" the industry. To its credit, it has removed the ineffective and cost-increasing separate subsidiary restrictions from AT&T in its *Third Computer Inquiry*, and it has given AT&T some minimal pricing flexibility for some new services. More recently, FCC staff economists have strongly advocated more radical deregulatory actions (Haring and Kwerel 1986) along the lines suggested later in this chapter. Perhaps in response to these arguments the commission has proposed to examine various methods for achieving deregulation (FCC 1987).

On the other hand, the FCC has become much more active in imposing regulation on the BOC's, particularly with regard to separate subsidiary and cost-allocation requirements. And while the commission proposes to examine methods of deregulation of AT&T, it appears to favor a service-by-service approach (FCC 1987), in which a proposal to "streamline" regulation for a particular service could be held up indefinitely by arguments about the definition of the service (remember Execunet?), and what costs are to be allocated to that service (remember Telpak?).

The FCC's real contribution can be reduced to two specific actions: eliminating the access subsidy and ensuring pricing based on historic accounting costs. While the first is quite laudable and the second dubious, neither has anything to do with deregulation.

An Immodest Proposal

Fifty years ago, to ease the pain of market failure, we took the analgesic of telecommunications regulation. Today, our nation is addicted to it and can't seem to break the habit that is sapping the strength of one of our most vital industries. Our leaders mouth the rhetoric of the reformed addict, but they have yet to put away the needle for good.

It is time for the regulation junkies to go cold turkey.

As long as there exist agencies, courts, or commissions who can exercise discretionary power to distribute the wealth of telecommunications among contending parties, they will be supported in their habit by the players of the regulatory game, the beneficiaries of inefficiency.

What we need is to rid telecommunications of regulation— not "regulatory reform," not "managed transition," and surely not "managed competition." The discretionary power to distribute wealth must be removed, and its removal cannot be left to the regulators. The drug of power is too strong to expect the addict to walk away from it.[3]

How can telecommunications regulation be abolished? Since the industry has both federal and state regulators, as well as the regulation of Judge Greene and the Justice Department, it would appear that the only legally feasible means is by federal legislation. Setting aside the political likelihood of such legislation, it will take an act of Congress to relieve the country and the telecommunications industry of its regulators.

But wouldn't immediate telecommunications deregulation hurt a lot of people? And what about those market failures, won't they still be there? What's to be done about them?

Direct Winners and Losers from Deregulation

Any major social change has immediate and direct impact on people, in the form of both gains and losses, as a rule, unequally distributed. As a first approximation, we can identify the broad categories of players who will gain and those who will lose.

Consumers, from large institutions down to the occasional-use residence customer, will be winners if they have their choice of suppliers and losers if they do not. Those who use lots of long-distance will be winners, and those who use little or no long-distance will be losers. Those who live in urban or suburban areas will be winners, and those in rural areas are likely to be losers.

Suppliers, including interconnect firms, competitive carriers, resellers, STS operators, bypassers, and network equipment suppliers, who operate with little restriction in markets today will gain little and may lose much. Those firms, including resellers, whose operation depends critically on restrictions that are lifted stand to lose everything. Suppliers such as AT&T and the BOC's who operate with substantial restriction may gain or lose, depending on the postderegulation strategies and competitors: If the lifting of restrictions allows the supplier to compete successfully in new markets, it's a winner; if lifting restrictions enables competitors to compete successfully in markets the supplier previously dominated, it's a loser. Suppliers who depend on use of the BOC local distribution network may lose if the BOC's deny or restrict access.

The reasons for these gains and losses are varied. Consumers without vendor choices will lose because some telecommunications markets remain monopolized, and competition may take some years to develop. Consumers who are the beneficiaries of today's subsidies will also lose. Firms who have benefited either directly or indirectly from restrictions on the BOC's or AT&T will lose an advantage when their competitor is no longer artificially handicapped. But firms that depend on the use of the bottleneck access line may lose through BOC refusals to deal.

Which Losses Really Hurt?

In principle, the benefits of deregulation should be plentiful enough so that everyone can be a winner. Practically, such equitable payoffs are not possible, and there will no doubt be some pain to distribute. Politically, of course, we would expect the best-organized and most influential parties to end up winners; this, in fact, is the story of the regulatory game. But beyond the political horse trading, what would be a reasonable set of postderegulation economic and social priorities?

First Priority: Consumers should not be subject to monopoly price gouging.

Corollary: Competitors should not have their access to bottleneck facilities restricted.

Second Priority: Currently subsidized consumers should be gradually but completely weaned from below-cost rates.

Last Priority: Firms that may lose a competitive advantage because of the relaxation of restrictions on others need no more consideration than they would receive in a competitive market. The stockholders and employees of firms that have entered the market in the last decade have lived with the uncertainty of the regulatory process. They didn't complain when it worked for them, and they can have no legitimate complaint when it works against them. Firms that cannot cut it in a competitive telecommunications market deserve not our sympathy but a quick and sure demise.

Long-Term Impact of Deregulation

Of course, in the longer term, the benefits of the competitive marketplace would be felt by all consumers. Alternate suppliers of local, long-distance, and CPE would find ways to reach more and more consumers as the obviously profitable markets reached saturation. Rural subscribers would benefit from the development of new technology, spurred by the removal of subsidies, that decreased their access costs. Consumers with little long-distance demand could still benefit from entry by local service providers (STS operators) that brought new services and technology to the home.

More to the point, the long-term benefits and costs of deregulation are almost always difficult to predict. In the case of the airline industry, the major fear prederegulation was that small towns would lose air service. In fact, overall service to small towns held steady, although new entrants into those markets tended to use prop planes rather than jets. The real results of deregulation (Bailey, Graham, and Kaplan 1985) had either not been predicted or not been believed before the CAB opened up the market:

Airlines went to the more efficient "hub-and-spoke" operation (routes centering on a major city) that reduced their costs;
Planes spent more time in the air, with more of their seats filled—capacity utilization jumped;
Air fares dropped to the point where many people who had never flown before could now afford it; and
Inflated salaries nosedived—pilots making $120,000 per year found that the new airlines could draw on a vast reserve of potential pilots who were willing and able to work for $40,000 per year.

The result: more passengers, more passenger-miles, and lower overall real costs.

Now, economists had predicted efficiency gains from airline deregulation, but no one had been able to pinpoint exactly how and why they would occur. Similarly, in telecommunications the long-term impact of deregulation will be better service, lower costs, and more technology. How, when, and why these will occur we cannot know until they happen.

Market Failures and Solutions

In Chapter 6, market failure was given as the economic rationale for public regulation of telecommunications. In particular, natural monopoly and the network externality, or universal-service objective, were the two market failures that prompted regulatory intervention. If deregulation occurs, won't these market failures return? If they are still a threat, can we find the means to control them without regulation?

In both cases, the answer is yes.

The network externality, the fact that a communications network is more valuable the more people are connected to it, was extremely important in the development of the system. Since the 1960s, the number of households connected to the network has approached a saturation level of over 90 percent, and the monthly price of subscription has stabilized at about the price of a large pizza. Despite the dire predictions of state regulators that the FCC's subscriber line charge of $2.00 per month would cause thousands to leave the network, its actual implementation in 1986 was greeted by consumers with a big yawn.[4] The notion that if subscribers were asked to pay the true cost of connecting them to the system, they would drop off the network is patently absurd. Of course, in rural areas those costs are substantially more than in urban and suburban areas. But an informal measure of country dwellers' willingness to pay for communications access can be seen by the high fraction of farms equipped with satellite antennas to receive TV signals. At today's costs and degree of household penetration and based on consumer response to the FCC's subscriber line charge, it is safe to say the network externality is no longer a significant market failure. The problem is small enough that it doesn't need a solution.

Monopoly power is not a small problem, however. The BOC's control the access line, which for the vast majority of subscribers and competitors is still a bottleneck facility. A deregulated BOC could offer long-distance service and give itself advantageous access compared to that of AT&T and the competitive carriers, or it could refuse to interconnect to STS operators, denying them access to the local distribution network.

A deregulated BOC could also increase rates to customers with no alternatives and extract monopoly profits. While competitive alternatives would develop eventually, price-gouging would almost certainly occur. A deregulated AT&T, on the other hand, could increase long-distance rates in those rural parts of the nation where MCI, Sprint, and others have no facilities. Since these routes are typically underpriced today, we would expect some increases, but the temptation to price-gouge beyond costs might be difficult for a sole supplier to resist.

The first problem relates to the withholding of access to a bottleneck facility, the access line, needed by other competitors. The next two problems relate to straight exploitation of monopoly power by the prices charged consumers. Solving these market-failure problems is a must if the first priority of deregulation is to be met. In the next section, we outline a solution that deals with each set of problems.

A Way Out?

In order to meet the two deregulation priorities (and the corollary) and solve the problems of monopoly power, we would have Congress add three crucial clauses to its bill mandating immediate deregulation.

One: in any market now served solely by AT&T or a BOC and designated as an essential monopoly, the rate charged by that firm for basic service can increase by no more than the annual increase in the Consumer Price Index (CPI). This cap would be in effect for a limited time, perhaps five years, after which the firm would be free to set the price wherever it wished. For example, if in 1988 the CPI increases by 3.5 percent, then local exchange companies could increase their rate for basic Dial Tone Line by 3.5 percent over what it had been in 1987. Their rates for CPE or Call Waiting would not be so constrained.

Two: equal access for all interexchange carriers under MFJ rules must be maintained. Further, all tariffs for access and local service must be nondiscriminatory and with no restrictions on resale and sharing.[5]

Three: all BOC carrier access charges, except those specifically incurred by the BOC to connect interexchange carriers to the local switch, are to be eliminated by the end of the five-year transition period, on a schedule to be determined by the BOC. The rate for carrier-incurred costs to the BOC would be indexed to the CPI.

Rate Indexing

The concept of indexing rates to the CPI as a means of controlling monopoly power is not new. Linhart and Radner (1984) suggested it as a means of deregulating AT&T. The Vermont Public Utility Commission introduced state legislation based on indexing sub-scription rates and deregulating everything else. Littlechild (Department of Industry 1983) recommended this approach upon the privatization of British Telecom, and the "RPI minus 3" rule (retail price index less 3 percent) has been adopted as a regulatory device by the British Office of Telecommunications: The average access price charged customers by British Telecom cannot increase in any one year at a rate greater than the rate of increase of the retail price index less 3 percent.

Indexing the price of services presently monopolized guarantees the consumer that today's rate, the best that regulation can do, will not increase in real terms for the five-year transition period. In fact, rate-indexing in this plan is not some form of automatic adjustment clause or a means of inducing productivity improvements, as suggested by Baumol (1982). Rather, its purpose is to grant a transitional insurance policy to subscribers who otherwise might be subject to price-gouging in markets temporarily monopolized by the existing carriers. In markets where price has been held below costs by regulation, rate-indexing will permit firms to use productivity gains to move prices closer to costs. If regulation has been effective in limiting price to below the monopoly level, then rate indexation guarantees to consumers that price will be stable during the transition to competition. In real terms, consumers could be no worse off during this transition period than they are today under traditional regulation.

The indexation rule should cap price increases in each market, not an average increase, as is the case with British Telecom. If AT&T's rates are indexed, for example, then the rate for a long-distance call could increase by no more than 3.5 percent, if that were the rate of CPI increase. AT&T would be free to deaverage its rates and perhaps even decrease the rate between one pair of cities at the same time it was increasing prices between other city-pairs within the same mileage band. Nor need AT&T increase all indexed rates by the same percentage in each year. But no market or service could experience a price increase greater than the rate of CPI increase. For each BOC, exchanges or parts of exchanges subject to STS competition would not be subject to the index cap. Basic subscription rates need not increase by the same percentage in each year. If a BOC or AT&T decreases an indexed rate one year, it can only increase it the next year subject to the CPI cap and cannot gain back the previous decrease all at once.

The level and quality of service today would have to be defined so that if AT&T or a BOC found the index cap inconvenient, it could not degrade service and thus reduce costs. Should AT&T or a BOC violate these service standards, the customer whose service had been degraded could sue for damages of, say, five times the monthly rate. Class-action suits would of course be permitted.

This plan raises a number of questions: what happens after five years? What if costs for a particular service increase faster than the CPI, so the BOC or AT&T loses money? What if there are great productivity gains so costs actually decline; won't the BOC or AT&T make excess profits? How about services now subsidized; won't the BOC's or AT&T object to having to provide them at a loss?

The answers are straightforward: in five years, those who have been receiving subsidies will have had ample time to be weaned; new suppliers will have time to prepare their market entry if they think they can do a better job. The BOC's and AT&T will have time to adjust their rates and their competitive strategies to a truly free market. If in the meantime the CPI cap rule causes a BOC or AT&T to lose money or to make excess profits, what of it? Firms in competitive markets often have losses or windfalls, depending on market circumstances; by what right do former monopolists or their customers claim insulation from such risk? And if the BOC's or AT&T object to continued subsidies for a transition period, how seriously should we take these transient troubles of the firms that are, after all, descendants of the principal architect of these subsidies?

Equal Access

The industry's experience with equal access suggests that it is fairly easy to define what equal access is and for the parties involved to monitor gross deviations from it. With deregulation, the BOC's would be permitted to offer long-distance service, including service from their own exchanges. Should they attempt to degrade access to their long-distance competitors, penalties could be set so that on showing disadvantage in court the offended carrier would be awarded some portion of the operating company's long-distance revenues for the period of disadvantage. Upon repeated convictions for restriction of access to long-distance competitors (for instance, five), the BOC could be enjoined from offering originating long-distance service or owning long-distance facilities in its own territory. It would be permitted, of course, to continue to offer long-distance service outside its territory and to complete calls to its own territory over lines leased from its competitors.

Removing resale restrictions and enforcing nondiscrimination by use or customer for monopoly services will prevent BOC's from throttling STS competition by restricting the STS operators' use of PBX trunks to BOC exchange switches. STS or other local service competitors will then be able to purchase PBX circuits to the BOC facilities on the same terms as a corporate customer, whose PBX serves only corporate employees. "Partitioning" the STS competitors' PBX's by end customer so that the BOC can discriminate by end-use, as is now required in Texas, would not be permitted. The results with nondiscriminatory WATS resale indicate that this will eliminate the incentive of the BOC's to restrict local service competitors' access to the local distribution network.

Phaseout of Carrier Access Charges

The core of the current FCC strategy regarding access is to remove the subsidy element from the carrier access charge and collect it as part of the subscriber line charge. The five-year phaseout of the carrier access charge also accomplishes this. However, the phaseout also includes the usage portion of the charge—why?

When an interexchange carrier requests a BOC to connect a group of its circuits to a local exchange switch, that carrier imposes connection costs on the BOC and should pay for those costs. However, when a customer originates a long-distance call using that exchange carrier, the cost to the BOC of transporting that call from the customer to the carrier is caused by the customer, not the carrier, and so should be recovered from the customer. Of course, the long-distance carrier can take the assignment of that rate, collecting it from the customer and reimbursing the BOC. If the BOC is prohibited from collecting the usage component of the access charge directly from the carrier, then it must recover it, directly or indirectly, from the customer. Obviously, the BOC should not be able to collect its usage costs from both the carrier and the customer.

Why Legislation?

If the plan is so good, why can't an enlightened regulator, in a spasm of good government such as seized the CAB in 1977, put it into practice? Why do we need to involve the U.S. Congress, which dealt so ineffectively with telecommunications regulation in the late 1970s and early 1980s?

Paradoxically, the difficulties Congress had in passing legislation offer a clue to the answers: Legislation, *once enacted*, tends to be rather permanent. Regulation, on the other hand, can always be reversed in the future, should one or more of the important players change their minds during the transition period. As long as regulators are present and capable of acting, there will always be pressures on them to favor some consumer group of some set of firms. Under such fire, the regulators' commitment to deregulation will most likely wilt. With the proposed legislation, however, the regulators disappear from this industry, and the lobbyists must look elsewhere to obtain special favors.

But wouldn't the lobbyists simply go back to Congress? Wouldn't the regulatory game now be played out on Capitol Hill? The lessons of the last congressional attempts with telecommunications suggest that there may indeed be much lobbying, but it would be unlikely to result in new legislation. It appears Congress is unwilling to change the status quo without consensus that change is a good thing. Legislation, it seems, is more stable than regulation. Apparently, the CAB deregulators of the late 1970s agreed; Alfred Kahn and his colleagues at the CAB lobbied hard for the Airline Deregulation Act of 1978, even though they were already actively deregulating at the board. The reasons: their achievements at the board could be easily toppled by their successors; legislation would be much, much harder to reverse.

If new legislation is so difficult to obtain, what are the prospects for this proposal? Rather dim, unfortunately. Although the rate-indexation scheme truly protects consumers during the transition to full competition, it does nothing to help the many firms — and entire industries — whose profitability is significantly enhanced by regulatory restrictions against AT&T and the BOC's. Permitting free-for-all competition may lower prices and increase benefits to consumers, but it will hurt firms that are not up to the competitive battles that will ensue. These firms will stand in the way of legislation that would bring the benefits of competition to consumers — all while claiming to be "protecting" the consumer! As was the case with airline deregulation, Congress may first need to be shown the way by bold regulators. Nebraska, Vermont, and Iowa all have commissions that have moved considerably faster than the FCC toward deregulation, and their successes may demonstrate that getting rid of regulators does not instantly result in consumer carnage.

The Payoff to Deregulation

Both AT&T and the BOC's would have to accept an unappealable cap on rate increases for monopoly services, in return for which *all* other restrictions on their operations would be lifted. Though the BOC's would be required to maintain equal access and no re-sale restrictions on monopoly local service, they would be free to compete with AT&T, and with each other, in the provision of long-distance service. AT&T, on the other hand, would be freed of regulation and could compete with the BOC's to provide local distribution facilities to its biggest and most profitable customers.

The consumer would merely have to sit back and enjoy the competition, as prices went down and service got better. AT&T, having already shown it can handle the small fry in the long-distance market, would get an opportunity to prove itself against seven tough, knowledgeable competitors. The BOC's, complacent with their regulatory defense of the monopoly access line, would soon find in AT&T and the other BOC's, competitors willing and able to pick off the cream of their markets. Finally, the offspring of Ma Bell would find worthy competitors: each other.

While competition in the mainstream markets would work to the consumers' advantage, what of the markets still monopolized? The guarantee of no price increase (in real terms) would ensure that the worst-off consumer could do no worse under indexation than under regulation.

What of the danger of the BOC's denying or restricting access to their bottleneck facilities? Of course, the best long-run solution would be to encourage competitive entry into access so that the facility would no longer be a bottleneck. In the short run, however, equal access and full resale of local facilities should ensure availability of BOC facilities to those competitors that need them. Experience with WATS resale and with the MFJ-mandated equal-access program suggests this will work.

But the biggest payoff by far will be the absence of the regulator. All restrictions of the proposed deregulation law are enforced by the individual parties, not by regulators. No need to complain of unfair competition; there will be no one to listen. No need to attempt to deny entry to your markets; there will be no one to enforce your restrictions. No need to "invent around" a regulation; there will be none. No need to hesitate to introduce an innovation fearing that an injured competitor will cry "Foul!"; there will be no one to heed the cry.

Conclusion

The last two decades have demonstrated that regulation of the telecommunications industry has been a failure, and yet we continue to look to the regulators to solve the problems of the industry. The lesson should be crystal clear: regulation will not solve these problems; regulation *is* the problem.

There is virtual consensus among thoughtful observers that it is vitally important to the national economy that this industry develop and grow where technology and consumers' needs take it.

There is virtual consensus that its past history of monopoly and regulation is the primary barrier to its development.

There is virtual consensus that "plain old telephone service" must be affordable for all Americans.

And so corporation heads, congresspersons, regulators, and judges have all tried their hand at solving this dilemma. With each attempt to cut the Gordian knot, the putative problem-solver, be it John deButts, Tim Wirth, or Judge Greene, has become part of the problem, yet another player in a regulatory game of unimaginable complexity.

It is time to stop throwing talent at this problem; history has demonstrated that the more people we have trying to solve it, the more difficult it becomes to solve.

It is now time to start taking people away from the problem. It is time to rely on the first and last resort of the American economic system: Let the market decide. Let consumers tell us which firms they want to deal with, which products they want, and how they want to use them. Let American technology work on increasing the choices for consumers, on undermining remaining market power through entrepreneurial innovation.

The system has been "fixed" too often; why don't we let it work like it's supposed to? Let's try it without the "fixers," for once!

Unfortunately, the political economy of the industry has been dominated by constant contention among aggressively self-serving participants. There is no reason to suspect that all or even most of the players would line up behind this deregulation proposal. Many firms, and some consumer groups, have been treated well by regulation and would be unwilling to give up their privileged position. But we have yet to hear from the most conspicuously absent party, who has found the complexities of the argument too tedious to become involved, but has the most at stake: the individual and institutional consumer.

It is time to send a clear message direct to Washington: We've had enough regulation, "unregulation," divestiture, antitrust, court suits, and catering to special interests. Americans deserve a telecommunications system as rich, diverse, and technologically exciting as their computer industry. Let's take away the regulators and let the market give us what we want. When the sleeping giant of the telecommunications-using public awakens and says to Congress, "Enough!," it will carry the day by *force majeure*. The special interests will scatter, the regulators will find other jobs, and we can get on with the business of creating and fulfilling our telecommunications needs for the twenty-first century.

Notes

1. The history of "inventing around" telecommunications regulations is a long one. In the early 1970s, the FCC's *(First) Computer Inquiry* established rules that kept the Bell System out of the growing computer business. AT&T immediately introduced the Dataspeed 40/4, which it called "terminal equipment"—therefore communications not computing—but which in fact possessed sub-

stantial (for the time) processing capability. AT&T used the Dataspeed 40/4 to test the *Computer Inquiry* rules to the limit, and it succeeded (Verveer 1984).

2. In a well-known case before the ICC, Southern Railway sought to introduce a new, cheaper boxcar for hauling agricultural commodities, the "Big John," planning to pass the savings thus realized on to its shippers in the form of lower rates. Although the ICC recognized this innovation as a "major break-through in the control of costs and a notable advance in the art of railroading" (ICC 1965), it nevertheless refused to allow Southern to pass on its full cost-savings out of concern for Southern's barge-line competitors. The ICC wished to "preserve for the barge line the cost advantage they enjoy with respect to certain port-to-port movements" (ICC 1963).

3. There are a few quite remarkable exceptions. Economists Alfred Kahn and his allies at the CAB not only deregulated the airlines but saw to the passage of legislation that abolished their agency, thus removing the locus of discre-tionary power that could attract seekers of favor. Less dramatically, the FCC's registration program for CPE deregulated that market (except for the BOC's), and the commission has been able to walk away from the regulation of that market without regret.

4. Even low-income customers did not respond; penetration in households earn-ing less than $5,000 per year held steady at about 71 percent from just before divestiture through 1986 (Pollack 1986).

5. During the limited transition period, firms now serving any market or service designated an essential monopoly would be required to file publicly available tariffs for those markets or services to ensure compliance with the CPI index.

References

Bailey, E., D. Graham, and D. Kaplan. 1985. *Deregulating the Airlines*. Cambridge, Mass.: The MIT Press.

Baumol, W.J. 1982. "Productivity Incentive Clauses and Rate Adjustment for In-flation." *Public Utilities Fortnightly* (July 22): 11–18.

FCC. *Decreased Regulation of Certain Basic Telecommunications Services*, CC Docket 86-421, "Notice of Proposed Rulemaking" (January 9, 1987).

Haring, J., and E. Kwerel. "Competition Policy in the Post-Equal Access Market," FCC Discussion Paper (December 1, 1986).

ICC. *Grain in Multiple-Car Shipments—River Crossings to the South*, 318 ICC 641, 683 (1963).

———. *Grain in Multiple-Car Shipments—River Crossings to the South*, Second Re-port and Order of the Commission on Reconsideration, 325 ICC 752, 759–760 (1965).

Linhart, P., and R. Radner. 1984. "Deregulation of Long-Distance Telecommuni-cations." In *Policy Research in Telecommunications*, edited by V. Mosco. Norwood, N.J.: Ablex Publishing.

Lipsky, A. 1986. "Antitrust Without Apology." Paper presented at the 13th An-nual Conference of the European Association for Research in Industrial Economics, West Berlin, Germany, August 24–27, p. 4.

Department of Industry. 1983. *Littlechild Report.* February. London: HMSO.

MIS Week. 1985a. "State Deregulation: SW Bell Fights Shared Services." September 4, p. 32.

———. 1985b. "State Deregulation: US West Chips Away Shackles." July 17, p. 42.

Murphy, K.J. 1981. "A Synthesis of the Empirical Evidence on Demographic Telecommunications Consumption Patterns." August. AT&T. Mimeo.

Pollack, A. 1986. "Phone Rate Increases Found Below Dire Predictions of '84." *New York Times*, June 16, p. 2.

Schulze, C. 1977. *The Public Use of Private Interests.* Washington, D.C.: The Brookings Institution.

Verveer, P. 1984. "Regulation and the Access Problem: What's Happened and Where We Are Now." In *Telecommunications Access and Public Policy*, edited by M.A. Baughcum and G.R. Faulhaber, pp. 83–88. Norwood, N.J.: Ablex Publishing.

Index

Above 890 MC decision, 24–25, 27, 28, 31, 35 n. 1, 52, 64; and predatory pricing, 118; and systems integrity, 36 n. 5

Access, 15, 16, 72–76, 139; and Bell operating companies, 124, 125, 130–131, 140, 141, 154–156, 168, 169, 171–172, 174; charges, 89, 100, 101 n. 2, 113, 122–124, 127, 130–131, 132, 140, 171–172; and deregulation, 169; and divestiture agreement, 83, 88, 89, 90–92, 98, 100, 130, 132–134; and Federal Communications Commission, 74–75, 127, 130–131, 132, 140–141, 152, 163; future prospects, 154–156; and independent telephone companies, 101 n. 2, 147 n. 3; and Microwave Communications, Inc., 73–74, 76, 83, 123, 124; and private branch exchanges, 171; and rural areas, 147 n. 3, 162; and states 145–146; *see also* Long distance

Adoption externalities, 12, 13

Airline Deregulation Act of 1978, 172

Airline deregulation, 44, 45, 56 n. 14, 63, 166–167, 172, 176 n. 3

Alabama, 145

Allnet, 71

American Economic Review, 53

American Newspaper Publishers Association, 143–144, 162

American Telephone and Telegraph. *See* Access; AT&T-Communications; AT&T-Information Systems; AT&T-Long Lines; Bell Laboratories; Bell operating companies; Connecting arrangements; Consent decree; Cross subsidies; Divestiture agreement; Local telephone companies; Long distance; Predatory pricing; Regulation; State regulation agencies; Technology; Western Electric

Antitrust, xvii; and Bell operating companies, 156; and connecting arrangements, 115, 123; economics of, 115–125; private suits, 33, 60, 81–83, 115–125; U.S. Department of Justice suit against Bell, 60, 81–83, 115–125; and Western Electric, 8, 115

Antitrust Procedures and Penalties Act, 84–85

Apollo project, 10

Arkansas, 146, 147

AT&T-Communications, 129, 130–131, 132; and divestiture agreement, 137, 138, 139; marketing success, 151–153; and pricing, 140

AT&T-Information Systems, 129, 135; and competition, 135, 138–139; and divestiture, 137–139, 142

AT&T-Long Lines, 15, 130

AT&T President's Conference, 29

Audion, 3, 5, 19 n. 11

Automatic dialing, 18

Averch, Harvey, 53

Bailey, Elizabeth, 45, 54, 56 n. 7

Baumol, William, 53, 169

Baxter, William, 82, 83, 86, 88, 90, 91, 95, 96, 102 n. 6, 115

BBC, 14

Bell, Alexander G., 1

Bell Journal of Economics and Management Science, 53

Bell Laboratories, xvi, 7, 9–10, 33–34; and Bell name, 99; and consent decree, 23–24; and economic analyses, 53–54;

Bell Laboratories *(cont.)*
  primacy of, 47; and television, 12–13; work force, 19 n. 7
"Bell" name, 98, 99
Bell operating companies (BOC's), 83, 87–90, 92–93, 130; and access, 124, 125, 130–131, 140, 141, 154–156, 168, 169, 171–172, 174; and antitrust action, 156; and billing and collection, 100; and bypass, 154, 155; and coin phones, 134; and competition, 87, 88, 89, 125, 154–156; and cross subsidies, 155; and customer premises equipment, 99, 134–135, 136, 147 n. 5, 156–157, 162, 176 n. 3; and deregulation, 163, 165, 171, 173–174; and divestiture agreement, 83, 88, 94–96, 97–101, 136; and equipment suppliers, 115, 120–121, 135–136, 138; and Federal Communications Commission, 140, 147, 163; future prospects, 154–155; line of business waivers, 99–100; and long distance service, 97–98, 100, 129, 131, 132, 140, 141, 143, 147, 171; and mobile phones, 84; and private branch exchanges, 171; rates, 136, 168, 169, 170; and regulation, 92–93, 94, 154–155, 156, 158–159; return on equity, 136; and *Second Computer Inquiry*, 140, 142, 147 n. 5, 157; and shared tenant services, 132–133, 154, 155, 170, 171; and state regulation, 93, 97–98, 136, 137, 144–145, 155–156, 161
Bell of Pennsylvania, 112
Bellcomm, 10
Bernstein, M.H., 41–42
"Big John" boxcars, 176 n. 2
Billing and collection services, 100
Blaszak, James, 141
BOC's. *See* Bell operating companies
Brandeis, Louis, 41, 50, 115
Brauetigam, Ronald, 44–45, 51
Brennan, T., 88, 102 n. 7, 115
Breyer, Stephen, 66 n. 6
British Telecom, 169, 170
Brophy, T.F., 87
Brown, Charles, 76–78, 83–85, 86, 87, 90, 95–96, 102 n. 5, 139, 156
Bruce, Robert, 78 n. 1
Bryant, John W., 141
Building complexes, telephone service for, 132
Bypass, 137, 154, 155

Cable TV, 132
California, 145
Call Waiting rate, 168
Canadian Pacific, 160
Capital equipment: depreciation, 10–11; obsolescence, 9–10, 11
Carter administration, 54, 81
Carterphone case, 27–28, 29, 46, 115, 122
CBS, 99
Cellular mobile phone, 83–84, 134, 154
Centrex, 145
Chicago school of economics, 43
Chicago–St. Louis private line service, 31, 46
CI-1. *See First Computer Inquiry*
CI-2. *See Second Computer Inquiry*
CIT-Alcatel, 136
Civil Aeronautics Board (CAB), 40, 56 n. 7, 56 n. 14, 161, 172, 176 n. 3; mail subsidies, 111; price formula, 65; *see also* Airline deregulation
Clayton Act, 5
Coaxial cables, 9, 12
Coin phones, 59, 134
Collins Radio, 24
Colorado, 156, 162
ComKey, 79 n. 4
Communications Act of 1934, 61, 63, 68, 113
Computers, 66–67, 175–176 n. 1; and AT&T-Information Systems, 135, 138–139; and private branch exchanges, 129, 138–139; and telephone market, 129–130
Connecting arrangements, 28–30, 32; and antitrust, 115, 123; and costs, 171–172; and harm to network argument, 122, 123; and regulation, 55
Consent Decree, 8, 23–24, 33, 85
Consumer Communications Reform Act (CCRA), 61
Consumer groups, 98, 155
Consumer Price Index and indexing, 168–169
Cornell, Nina, 78 n. 1
Costs: Bell manual, 64–65; and Bell operating companies, 97–98; and connecting arrangements, 171–172; and entry, 91; FCC analysis, 25–26, 78 n. 2; and monopoly power, 106–108; non-traffic sensitive (NTS), 140; and pricing, 140, 142–143, 153; and rates, 15–16, 113; and regulation, 153

CPE. *See* Customer premises equipment
Cross licensing, 8–9, 13, 19 n. 16
Cross subsidies, 25–27; accountant solution, 64–65; and Bell operating companies, 155; and consent decree, 23–24; and Federal Communications Commission, 64–67, 115, 153; and monopoly economics, 108–109, 118–120; and specialized carriers, 32–33; structuralist solution, 65–67, 69–71; and U.S. Congress, 63–64, 67, 97
Customer premises equipment (CPE), 36 n. 4; and Bell operating companies, 99, 134–135, 136, 147 n. 5, 156–157, 162, 176 n. 3; and competition, 60, 135, 142; and divestiture, 83, 88, 89, 134–135, 136; and FCC registration, 59, 176 n. 3; independent, 135; future prospects, 156–157; and key systems, 157; and predatory pricing, 118, 122; and private branch exchanges, 157; rates, 168; and refusal to deal, 122–123; regulation, 156; subsidization of other services, 109

Data processing, 129–130, 157
Data sets, 28
Data transmission, 13, 51–52; codes and protocols, 156–157
Dataspeed 40/4, 175–176
Datran, Inc., 50–52
DeButts, John, 61–63, 76, 78, 174
DeForest, Lee, 3, 5, 19 n. 11
Deregulation, 162–175; and access, 169; airlines, 44, 45, 56 n. 14, 63, 166–167, 172, 176 n. 3; and Bell operating companies, 163, 165, 171, 173–174; and consumers, 164–166; long-term effects, 166–167; and market failures, 167–168; and marketing, 130–131; and rural telephones, 166, 167–168; and shared tenant services, 165, 166; and suppliers, 165; and U.S. Congress, 95, 172–173; *see also* Regulation
Dial Tone Line rate, 168–169
Digital Equipment Corporation, 138, 139
Digital transmission, 51–52
Direct Distance dialing, 33
Divestiture agreement: and access, 83, 88, 89, 90–92, 98, 100, 130, 132–134; and AT&T-Communications, 137, 138, 139; and AT&T-Information Systems, 137–139, 142; and Bell operating companies, 83, 88, 94–96, 97–101, 136; and customer premises equipment, 83, 88, 99, 134–135, 136; failure, probabilities for, 89–96; and Federal Communications Commission, 86, 89, 90, 94–95, 139–143, 144; and local phone companies, 132–134, 141; and long distance, 83, 88–89, 90–92, 127, 130–132; and marketing, 130–131; and monopoly, 90–92; and state regulators, 56 n. 8, 128, 144–146; success, probabilities for, 87–89; and systems integration, 128–130; and U.S. Congress, 85–87, 90, 97; and U.S. Department of Justice, xvi–xvii, 83–84, 87–96, 97, 143; and Western Electric, 135–136, 138, 139
Dole, Robert, 143–144
DUV tariff, 52

Eckstein, Otto, 53
Economics: and antitrust, 115–125; Bell analyses, 53–54; and Federal Communications Commission, 50, 53, 163; and monopoly, xvii, 105–125; and regulation, xvii, 42–44, 48–49, 105–115, 162–163
Edison, Thomas A., 1
Efficiency: and monopoly, 112; and regulation, 44–45, 108, 112, 153, 155, 156, 157, 158–175
Eisenhower administration, 8
Electric utilities, 44
Electronic publishing, 98, 99, 144, 162
Emerson, 12
ENFIA. *See* Exchange Network Facilities for Interstate Access
Engineering standards, 29–30
English, William, 141
Entry, xv, 29; and costs, 91; and economics of monopoly, 109; and Federal Communications Commission, 48–52, 54–55; and regulation, xvi, 6, 10, 18, 23, 46, 47, 48–49, 156, 158, 161–162; and technology, 10–11
Equipment suppliers, 115, 120–121, 135–136, 138
Ericcson, 136
Exchange Network Facilities for Interstate Access (ENFIA), 73–76, 123–124, 141; discount, 131; and Microwave Corporation, Inc., 146
Execunet service, 68–69, 73–74, 123–124

Federal Communications Commission (FCC), xv, 7–8; and access, 74–75, 127, 130–131, 132, 140–141, 152, 163; and Bell operating companies, 140, 147, 163; and Carterphone, 27–28; and connecting devices, 29–30, 32; cost analyses, 25–26, 78 n. 2; and cross subsidy, 64–67, 115, 153; and customer premises equipment, 59, 176 n. 3; and Datran, 50–52; and divestiture agreement, 86, 89, 90, 94–95, 139–143, 144; economists, 50, 53, 163; engineering standards, 29–30; and entry, 48–52, 54–55, and key systems, 59; and long distance subsidization of local service, 140, 152; and Microwave Communications, Inc., 49, 51, 115, 118; and microwave transmission, 24; and pricing, 163; and private branch exchange, 59, 67–68; and public policy, 112–115; and rates, 26–27; registration program, 59–60; scope of regulation, 56 n. 8; and television transmission, 12–13, 23; and terminal equipment, 55; and volume discounts, 113; and WATS service, 69–71
Federal Trade Commission, 40
Ferejohn, J.A., 42
Ferris, Charles, 65–66
Fiber optics, 91, 152
Field, Stephen J., 39
Fiorina, M.P., 42
First Computer Inquiry (CI-1), 66, 175–176 n. 1
"500" telephone, 10
Food and Drug Administration, 41
Forward-looking incremental costs accounting, 75–76, 143
Fowler, Mark, 163
Freidheim, Jerry W., 144
Fully separated subsidiaries (FSS), 66–67

Gaskins, Darius, 56
General Electric, 8, 128
Gordon, Myron, 53
Graham, D.R., 45
Greene, Harold, xvi–xvii, 81–83, 84–85, 96–101, 115, 125, 128, 136, 143–144, 147, 152, 153, 162, 174
GTE, 86, 136

Hadley, A.T., 55 n. 2
"Hi-Lo" tariff, 32
Historical costs, 142–143
Hush-a-Phone case, 49

IBM, 13, 28, 77, 129; communications systems, 128, 139; litigation, 85, 101 n. 1, 102 n. 6; and long distance service, 132, 152; and videotext, 99
Illinois, 145
Illinois Bell, 61, 62
"Impact" program, 62–63
Income distribution and regulation, 41
Independent telephone companies: and access, 101 n. 2, 147 n. 3; acquisition by Bell, 3–5, 6, 17; and consumer premises equipment, 135; and long distance, 17; market share, 2; and regulation, 46
Indiana, 145
Installation fees, 15
Intercom services, 132
Interconnection. *See* Connecting arrangements
Interstate Commerce Commission (ICC), 5–6, 7, 40, 42; and boxcar innovation, 176 n. 2; price formula regulation, 65, 148 n. 8
Iowa, 173
Irwin, Manley, 50
IT&T, 136

Jarvis, Howard, 43
Johnson, Leland L., 53

Kahn, Alfred E., 44, 53, 54, 56 nn. 6 and 7, 172, 176 n. 3
Kansas, 147
Kaplan, D.P., 45
Kennedy, Edward, 63
Key systems, 28, 30; competition, 79 n. 4; and customer premises equipment, 157; and Federal Communications Commission, 59; new entrants, 60; and Western Electric, 136
Kingsbury, J.E., 18 n. 6
Kingsbury Commission, 6, 17, 18–19 n. 6
Knight-Ridder newspapers, 99
Kolko, Gabriel, 42
Kreps, D., 125

"Leaky switch" problem, 36 n. 5
Least-cost long-distance service, 131
Lexitel, 71
Linhart, P., 169
Lipsky, Abbott, 159, 163
Littlechild, 169
Loading coils, 2, 5

Local Access and Transport Area (LATA), 98–99; intra traffic, 129, 131, 145–146, 152, 160
Local loops. *See* Access
Local phone companies: competition, 97; and divestiture, 132–134, 141; and long distance connection, 15–18, 72–76, 82, 98–99; subsidization of rates, 89, 97, 100, 111, 123–124, 140, 162
Locke, John, 39
Long, Huey P., 56 n. 4
Long distance, 2–3, 68–69; and Bell operating companies, 97–98, 100, 129, 131, 132, 140, 141, 143, 147, 171; billing and collection, 100; competition, 153; and divestiture, 83, 88–89, 90–92, 127, 130–132; future prospects, 151–154; and IBM, 132, 152; and local phone companies, 15–18, 72–76, 82, 98–99; and Microwave Communications, Inc., 68–69, 73–74, 76, 88, 118, 130, 151, 168; pricing, 112–113, 118, 122–123; subsidization of local phone companies, 89, 97, 100, 111, 123–124, 140, 162
Lowry, E.D., 106

MacAllister, Jack, 137
MacAvoy, P.W., 41
McGovern, William, 141
Magnetic inductance coil, 18 n. 1
Market failure, 106–115, 167–168
Marketing, 10, 36 n. 7, 76–77; and divestiture, 130–131
Massachusetts Board of Railroad Commissioners, 40
Mayhew, D.R., 42
MCI. *See* Microwave Communications, Inc.
Megacom services, 134, 154
Melody, Bill, 50
Message Telephone Service (MTS), 68; and WATS, 69, 131
Microwave transmission, 9, 12; and Federal Communications Commission, 24; private companies, 24–25, 30–33, 50–52; and television, 12–13
Microwave Communications, Inc. (MCI), 30–31, 34, 64, 77; and access, 73–74, 76, 83, 123, 124; antitrust suit against Bell, 33, 146; and Federal Communications Commission, 49, 51, 115, 118; long distance service, 68–69, 73–74, 76, 88, 118,

130, 151, 168; market share, 151, 153; and regulation, 46, 52, 55, 86, 146; return on equity, 131; and WATS lines, 71
Milgrom, P., 125
Mill, John Stuart, 106
Mobile phones, 83–84, 134, 154
Modification of Final Judgment (MFJ), 85, 97, 102 n. 7; *see also* Divestiture agreement
Monopoly: and access, 92; and costs, 106–108; and cross subsidy, 108–109, 118–120; economics of, xvii, 105–125; and efficiency, 112; and entry, 109; natural, 106–109; and pricing, 108–109, 110–111, 112–113, 115–120
Monthly service charge, 17, 24
Morgan, J.P., 2
Morse, A., 60
Motorola, 36 n. 3
Mountain Bell, 162
Munn v. Illinois, 39

Nader, Ralph, 43
National Academy of Science, 30
Nebraska, 137, 145, 173
NEC, 136
Network externality, 110–112, 113; and deregulation, 167–168
New Deal and regulation, 40–41
New Jersey, 145
New York state, regulation, 6
New York Central, 24
New York Public Service Commission, 19 n. 13
Newspaper industry and electronic publishing, 98, 99, 143–144, 147
North American Telecommunications Association, 162
Northern Telecom, 136

O'Brien, Bradley, 134
Olivetti, 135
Olsen, James, 139
Olympic & York, 147
OlympiaNet, 147 n. 4
Ontario, Canada, 159–161
Ontario Highway Transport Board, 160
Oregon, 137, 145
Owen, B.M., 44–45, 51

Patents, 1–2, 33–34, 92; and consent decree, 23–24; trading of, 10

PBX. *See* Private branch exchanges
PC6300 personal computer, 135
Peltzman, S., 42
Pennsylvania Pub. Util. Comm'n v. Bell Tel. Co. of Pa., 19 n. 9
Perspective Telecommunications Group, 134
Philco, 12, 23, 47–48
Philips, 136
Picturephone, 19 n. 13
Posner, R., 42
Power, Patrick, 145
Predatory pricing, 26–27, 29, 118, 123; multiperiod, 125 n. 2; against specialized carriers, 32–33, 36 n. 3, 115; subsidizing of, 115–120; and U.S. Congress, 97; *see also* Pricing
Pricing: and AT&T Communications, 140; and costs, 140, 142–143, 153; and Federal Communications Commission, 163; and long distance, 112–113, 118, 122–123; and monopoly theories, 108–109, 110–111, 112–113, 115–120; and regulation, 46–47, 107–108, 142–143; *see also* Predatory pricing
Private branch exchanges (PBX), 28, 30; and Bell operating companies, 171; and computing, 129, 138–139; and cross subsidy, 66–67; and customer premises equipment, 157; and Federal Communications Commission, 59, 67–68; and interconnection, 66 n. 5; systems sales, 128–129; and WATS service, 20–21; and Western Electric, 66–67, 136
Process innovation, 9, 10
Product innovation, 9, 19 n. 13
Protectionism, 157
Pupin & Campbell, 3, 5
Producer-protection theory of regulation, 42
Progressive Era, 40
Public policy issues, 112–115

Quick Action Collection Co. v. New York Tel. Co., 19 n. 9

Radio, 8–9, 12
Radio Corporation of America (RCA), 8, 12, 13
Radner, R., 169
Railroad regulation, 39–40, 42, 148 n. 8
Ramsay pricing, 108, 109, 112–113

Rates: arbitrage, 69–71, 131; and Bell operating companies, 136, 168, 169, 170; caps on, 168–170, 173; and customer premises equipment, 168; and deregulation, 168; FCC study, 26–27; indexing, 168–170, 173; local, 15–16, 113, 168–169; and regulators, 56 n. 8, 69–71, 107–108, 152; and rural telephone service, 46, 47, 152, 153, 162; and specialized carriers, 32, 69–71; and state regulators, 98, 144–146
Raytheon, 12, 23, 47–48
Reagan administration, 82, 95–96
Refusal to deal, 121–125
Regional holding companies, 135, 137, 142; line of business waivers, 143
Regulation, 5–8, 23–35; Bell's compact with, 45–48; and Bell operating companies, 92–93, 94, 154–155, 156, 158, 159; and competition, 86–87; and computers, 152, 157; and connecting arrangements, 55; and costs, 153; and customer premises equipment, 156; and divestiture, 92–93, 94–96, 139–147; economics of, xvii, 42–44, 48–49, 105–115, 162–163; and efficiency, 44–45, 108, 112, 153, 155, 156, 157, 158–175; and entry, xvi, 6, 10, 18, 23, 46, 47, 48–49, 156, 158, 161–162; future prospects of industry, 157, 158–159; history of, 39–45; and income distribution, 41; indirect damages, 161–162; inventing around, 160–161, 175–176 n. 1; judicialization, 44–45; lifecycle of, 41–42; and market failure, 106–115; and Microwave Communications, Inc., 46, 52, 55, 86, 146; and monopoly economics, 105–115; political scientists' critique, 41–43; and price, 46–47, 107–108, 142–143; and public interest, 112–115, 146; and shared tenant services, 158, 161; and separations and settlements, 56 n. 8, 114; and special interests, 42–43; supply side, 42; *see also* Deregulation; State regulation agencies
Roberts, J., 125
Rockefeller, John D., 5, 6
Rohlfs, J.H., 111
Rolm, 77
"RPI minus 3" rule, 169
Rural Electrification Administration, 56 n. 9
Rural telephone service: and access, 147 n. 3, 162; and cellular mobile phone, 154;

Rural telephone service *(cont.)*
and deregulation, 166, 167–168; and rate averaging, 46, 47, 152, 153, 162; subsidization of, 111–112, 114–115, 127, 162

San Francisco peace conference, 12
Satellite Business Systems (SBS), 152
Scanlon, J.J., 53
Scher, S., 42
Schmitt, Harrison, 67
Schulze, Charles, 162
Sears Roebuck, 99
Second best, economic theory of, 107–108
Second Computer Inquiry (CI-2), 66–67, 69, 71, 86; and Bell operating companies, 140, 142, 147 n. 5, 157; and data transmission, 157; and systems sales, 129, 138
Securities Exchange Commission, 40
Separations and settlements, 15–18, 27, 46, 72; and divestiture, 89; and regulation, 56 n. 8, 114
"Series 11,000" tariff, 32
"Seven Way Cost Study," 25–26, 64–65
Shared tenant services (STS), 132–133, 146–147, 154; and Bell operating companies, 132–133, 154, 155, 170, 171; and deregulation, 165, 166; and regulation, 158, 161
Sidley & Austin, 83, 85
Siemens, 136
Smith, Adam, 39, 41
Smith v. Illinois Bell Telephone Co., 15, 16–17, 34, 75
Solid-state physics, 33, 34
Southern Railway, 176 n. 2
Southwestern Bell, 146–147, 148 n. 6, 156
Space program, 10
Specialized Common Carrier decision, 31–33, 51, 55, 64, 65, 68
Sprint, 55; and access, 71, 76, 83, 88; marketing, 130, 151
Stalon, Charles, 146
State regulation agencies, 6; and access, 145–146; and Bell operating companies, 93, 97–98, 136, 137, 144–145, 155–156, 161; and divestiture, 56 n. 8, 128, 144–146; and local service subsidy, 89, 93, 98; and long distance, 145; and rates, 98, 144–146; scope of regulation, 56 n. 8
Stigler, G., 42
Stromberg-Carlson, 136

STS. *See* Shared tenant services
Sunk costs, 91, 106, 134
Switching: costs, 133; equipment, 89, 135–136, 138; future prospects, 157–158; protectionism, 157–158; technology, 9, 152
Systems engineering, 9, 10

TD-2 system, 24, 52
Technology, xvi, 8–11, 33, 47; control and competition, 6–7, 9, 23, 33–35; and entry, 10–11; licensing of, 8; and long distance, 2–5, 152; and monopoly, 47–48; and regulation, 47–48; and television, 11–14; timing of introduction, 9–10, 47
Telecommunications consultants, 59–60, 129
Telephone stamps, 114
Telephones, 10, 27–30, 46; connecting devices, 49; mobile, 83–84, 134, 154
Television and Bell system, 11–14, 23, 33
TELPAK tariff, 24–25, 27, 31, 36 nn. 3 and 6, 79 n. 7; and predatory pricing, 118, 123; and rate of return, 26
Terminal equipment, 35; competition, 27–30, 32; and Federal Communications Commission, 55; as marketing device, 36 n. 7
Texas, regulation, 19 n. 8, 171
Third Computer Inquiry, 139, 140, 157, 163
3B processes, 135, 138–139
Time, 93
Transfer pricing, 120–121
Transistors, 23, 33–34
Transmission equipment, 89, 135–136; future prospects, 157–158; protectionism, 157–158
Truman, Harry S., 12
Tukey, John, 53
Tunney Act, 85, 96–97, 98

United Parcel Service, 159
United States v. Standard Oil, 5
United States v. Western Electric Company et al., 8
U.S. Congress, xv, 61–64, 67, 81, 102 n. 5; and access charges, 141; and airline deregulation, 172; and cross subsidy, 63–64, 67, 97; and deregulation, 95, 172–173; and divestiture agreement, 85–87, 90, 97; and predatory pricing, 97; and subsidization of local service, 127
U.S. Department of Defense, 128

U.S. Department of Justice: and antitrust suit against Bell, 60, 81–83, 115–125; consent decree, 8, 23–24, 33; divestiture agreement, xvi–xvii, 83–84, 87–96, 97, 142; and IBM, 101 n. 1; *see also* Antitrust; Consent decree; Divestiture agreement; Western Electric

U.S. Supreme Court, 28, 39, 68–69

U.S. West, 137, 156

United Telecommunications, 147

Universal service goal, 6, 14, 18, 78; and network externality, 110–112, 113–114; and rates, 24; and regulation, 34, 48

University Computing Corporation, 51

Vacuum tube, 3

Vail, Theodore, 2–5, 24, 139; acquisition strategy, 5–7, 17; and local service, 16; and regulation, 5–7, 8, 11, 13, 139, 45–48

Van Deerlin, 61, 63, 67

VAX, 139

Vermont, 145, 169, 173

Verveer, Phil, 65–66, 69–70

Videotext, 98, 99, 144, 147

Volume discounts, 113

Von Auw, Alvin, 54

Waddy, Judge, 85

Walker, Paul A., 7–8, 33

WATS service, 13, 134, 174; and Federal Communications Commission, 69–71; and Microwave Communications, Inc., 71; technology, 152

Wein, Harold, 53

Wenders, J.T., 133

Western Electric; and antitrust action, 8, 115; and consent decree, 23; and divestiture, 135–136, 138, 139; and key systems, 136; and private branch exchanges, 66–67; and regulation, 7

Western Union, 25, 36 n. 3

Westinghouse, 8, 13

Wilson, James Q., 43

Wilson, R., 125

Wirth, Tim, 63, 67, 86, 97, 102 n. 6, 174

Wisconsin, regulation, 6

Word processing, 129

Wyoming, 99

Yellow Pages, 83, 98, 99, 100, 125, 136, 148 n. 6

Zenith, 12

About the Author

Gerald R. Faulhaber is associate professor of public policy and management at The Wharton School, University of Pennsylvania, and has been director of Wharton's Fishman–Davidson Center for the Study of the Service Sector since 1984. Previously, he was director of strategic planning and financial management at American Telephone and Telegraph Co., following his assignment as AT&T's director of microeconomic studies in 1978. Prior to his career at AT&T, Dr. Faulhaber was research head, Economic and Financial Research Department at Bell Laboratories, Inc. He is a co-editor of *Telecommunications Access and Public Policy* and *Services in Transition: The Impact of Information Technology on the Service Sector* (Ballinger 1986). In addition, he has published numerous papers and has served as referee for the *American Economic Review, Econometrica,* and the *Journal of Political Economy.* Dr. Faulhaber holds an A.B. in mathematics from Haverford College, an M.S. in mathematics from New York University, and an M.A. and a Ph.D. in economics from Princeton University.